D0331316

THE CHARACTERS

LU HUA, political instructor of a company of the Chinese People's Liberation Army

LU TA-CHENG, company commander

CHEN HSI, Third Platoon leader

CHAO TA-TA, Eighth Squad leader

HUNG MAN-TANG, old mess officer

TUNG AH-NAN, young recruit, formerly a student

MESSENGER

LIBERATION ARMY FIGHTERS

CHUN-NI, wife of Chen Hsi; model peasant who carries supplies of grain to the front

AH-HSIANG, flower girl, Ah-nan's elder sister

MAMA TUNG, mother of Ah-hsiang and Ah-nan

CHOU TEH-KUEI, veteran worker in a power plant; member of the Communist Party

AH-JUNG, son of Chou Teh-kuei; a boy who sells evening papers

LIN YUAN-YUAN, a girl student; schoolmate of Ah-nan and his girl friend

LO KE-WEN, Lin Yuan-yuan's cousin

MRS. LIN, Lin Yuan-yuan's mother

FAT MA, maid of the Lin family

CHU MAN-LI, Lin Yuan-yuan's classmate; a Kuomintang secret agent disguised as a student

FEIFEI, a hooligan

OLD K, head of the Kuomintang secret agents on the Nanking Road

OLD SEVEN, Old K's right-hand man

NURSES

THUGS

AMERICAN REPORTER

NUNS

WELL-DRESSED WOMAN and HER HUSBAND

A CAPITALIST and WIFE

MAN WEARING GLASSES and WIFE

ICE-CREAM VENDOR

MEAT-DUMPLING VENDOR

DANCE-HALL HOSTESS

BROKER

SHOE-SHINE BOY

PASSERS-BY

BRITISH, AMERICAN and JAPANESE SOLDIERS

GIRL STUDENTS

AH-NAN'S FATHER

DEMONSTRATORS

A Stage View of the Nanking Road

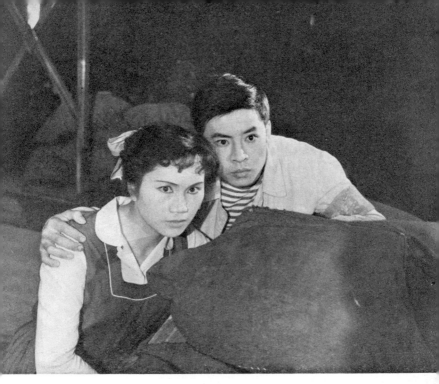

Scene One

Scene One

Scene Two

Scene Two

Scene Four

Scene Seven

Scene Seven

Scene Eight

Scene Nine

Scene Nine

SCENE ONE

A misty night in mid-summer.
The Nanking Road in Shanghai.
Guns boom sporadically.

TUNG AH-NAN, cautiously rising from behind a barricade in the street, turns and whistles. LIN YUAN-YUAN dashes over to him, looking very worried.

AH-NAN: Lin Yuan-yuan!

YUAN-YUAN: Tung Ah-nan!

AH-NAN: Why are you so late?

YUAN-YUAN: Mother locked me in. Fortunately, the maid helped me to escape. Where are the others from the Students' Union?

AH-NAN: They left some time ago and went with Uncle Chou to welcome the Liberation Army. I stayed behind to wait for you.

YUAN-YUAN: Then let's hurry!

AH-NAN (*stopping*): Someone's coming.

YUAN-YUAN: Is it the Liberation Army?

AH-NAN: I can't see.

YUAN-YUAN: Is it my mother or my cousin?

AH-NAN: It doesn't look like them.

(They drop out of sight behind the barricade. A little later they look out again.)

YUAN-YUAN: I'm scared, Tung Ah-nan....

AH-NAN: What? You're sorry you've come?

YUAN-YUAN: No, but I'm afraid if I run into mother she'll force me to go to America.

AH-NAN: Then go to my house and hide there.

YUAN-YUAN: No. See these gifts; I want to give them to the Liberation Army men myself.

(*Rifle shots off-stage.*)

AH-NAN: Ssh! Get down!

(*Three thugs, escorting OLD K who is dressed in a Kuomintang military uniform, move furtively along the street.*)

OLD K: Keep an eye open to see if someone's following us!

(*OLD SEVEN comes out of a tall building to greet them.*)

OLD SEVEN: Director Ma!

OLD K: Ssh! From now on I'm to be known as Mr. K.

OLD SEVEN: This way please, Mr. K. A sampan's waiting for you on the Huangpu River.

OLD K: Plans have been changed. The Americans want us to go underground.

OLD SEVEN: Go underground?

OLD K: We're to see that within three months the Reds turn black and rot right here on the Nanking Road. (*Goes into the building.*)

OLD SEVEN: Very good!

(*The thugs follow OLD K into the building. AH-NAN bounds over the barricade and shadows them. LIN YUAN-YUAN follows him.*)

YUAN-YUAN: Let's hurry!

AH-NAN: No! I don't know where those fellows come from! Yuan-yuan, go and get in touch with the Liberation Army; I'll keep an eye on those men.

2

YUAN-YUAN: All alone?

AH-NAN: I can cope with them. You run along now.

(*Off-stage, LO KE-WEN calls:* "*Yuan-yuan!*")

YUAN-YUAN: My cousin's coming!

(*They hide behind the barricade.*)

(*Dressed in a neatly pressed Western suit, LO KE-WEN appears carrying a violin case in one hand and a suitcase in the other. MRS. LIN, a plump middle-aged woman, wearing a long gown and high-heeled shoes, follows him.*)

MRS. LIN: Can you see her anywhere, Ke-wen?

LO (*shrugging*): She disappeared right in front of my eyes.

MRS. LIN (*sobbing*): ... If I don't find my daughter, I'm done for!

LO: Stop snivelling, Aunt! Your crying upsets me.

MRS. LIN: You really are hopeless, Ke-wen! You can't even keep watch on a young girl.

LO: I refuse to believe my cousin has the courage to abandon us and go over to the Communists. Her singing is nearly as good as Western vocalists. Success in her art is already in sight. It's unimaginable that she'll give up like this and waste her life! Absolutely unimaginable!

MRS. LIN: Instead of talking nonsense, you had better hurry up and look for her!

(*AH-NAN pops out from behind the barricade.*)

AH-NAN: Hey! No thoroughfare!

MRS. LIN (*startled*): Oh! How you scared me!

LO (*regaining his composure*): So it's you!

MRS. LIN: Who's he?

3

LO: One of those poor students from the Students' Union. He used to work as a docker and a shoe-shine boy on the Nanking Road.

AH-NAN: D'you want your shoes shined?

MRS. LIN: He looks like one of Yuan-yuan's classmates.

AH-NAN: I'm not good enough to be her classmate; we're not even in the same school. (*He vaults over the barricade.*)

MRS. LIN: That's right, but you belong to the same Students' Union. You were the one who took Yuan-yuan to the hunger demonstration that time!

AH-NAN: But when we were almost there, you came and brought her back.

MRS. LIN: Of course I did, because she wasn't hungry. The truth is, Ah-nan, that just in these difficult days my daughter has disappeared again.

AH-NAN: Is that so?

MRS. LIN: Yes. If you happen to see her....

AH-NAN: I'm sorry, but I haven't seen her.

LO: We'll gain nothing from a man like this, Aunt.

AH-NAN: It's safer for you at home, Madame! The Communists won't touch you when they come!

MRS. LIN: From the way you talk, you sound like a Communist yourself.

AH-NAN: I'm not qualified. (*Jumps back behind the barricade.*)

LO: How could the Communists want anyone like him? Let's go, Aunt!

(*LO KE-WEN continues towards the barricade.*)

AH-NAN: Hey! Be careful you aren't stopped by a stray bullet!

(*LIN YUAN-YUAN takes this opportunity to escape. LO KE-WEN sees her and gives chase. The thugs*

4

come out of the tall building. . . . They have changed into Liberation Army uniforms.)

THUG A: Who goes there? Put your hands up!

LO: Don't shoot! We're just ordinary people.

THUG A: Don't panic! We're Liberation Army men.

LO
MRS. LIN } (*flabbergasted*): Huh! Liberation Army men!
(*Turns to run.*)

THUG A: Why are you running away? Come back here! (*Moving towards them*) One of you wears glasses and the other high-heeled shoes. Both of you look like bad elements!
(*OLD K and OLD SEVEN appear in the doorway of the building.*)

MRS. LIN: We know how to mind our own business, Sir. . . . (*Recognizing OLD SEVEN*) Oh! Aren't you the owner of the Lili Dance Hall? Please put in a good word for me!

OLD SEVEN: Ah, Madame Lin! (*To OLD K*) She's an ordinary citizen who knows how to mind her own business, Comrade.

OLD K: Madame Lin? Why, it's this very kind of person the revolution is meant to be against. (*Signals with his eyes to the others.*)

THUG B (*pointing to the suitcase*):   What's this?

LO (*refusing to surrender it*):   A suitcase.

THUG A: You scoundrel! You're carrying ammunition in it!

LO: Nothing of the sort. It's money!
(*THUG A snatches the suitcase.*)

THUG A (*pointing to the violin case*):   What's this?

LO: A violin.

THUG A: What?

5

LO: A fiddle.

THUG A: I bet it's a machine-gun. (*Snatches it.*)

LO: You barbarians!

MRS. LIN: Forget it, Ke-wen. Let's go. (*Pulls LO KE-WEN along by the arm.*)

(*OLD K leads the thugs off.*)

(*AH-NAN suddenly stands in OLD K's way.*)

AH-NAN (*arms outstretched*): Oh, Liberation Army men. You've done a good job! I've come to welcome you.

OLD K: You're. . . .

AH-NAN: From the Students' Scout Team.

OLD K: So now we join forces.

AH-NAN: Right! Won't you come to our office for a rest?

OLD K: Sorry, I can't! We've other tasks.

OLD SEVEN: The comrades still have other affairs to attend to.

(*The thugs start to leave.*)

AH-NAN: Hey, be careful! Mines are planted over there!

(*OLD K and the others turn to go in another direction.*)

AH-NAN: There're mines over there too!

OLD K: Then will you please lead the way!

(*As AH-NAN turns to lead the way, OLD K strikes him with his fist. THUG A rushes up and beats AH-NAN unconscious.*)

OLD K: Finish him off and throw him in the gutter. Otherwise our plans for the Nanking Road will fall through and all the work we've done will be a waste of time.

(*OLD K and OLD SEVEN run off. THUGS A and B
drag AH-NAN away. LIN YUAN-YUAN shouts off-
stage: "Ah-nan! Tung Ah-nan!"*)

YUAN-YUAN: Tung Ah-nan! Ah-nan!... (*She goes
into the tall building.*)
(*Third Platoon Leader CHEN HSI enters with Squad
Leader CHAO TA-TA and several other fighters. LIN
YUAN-YUAN comes out of the building.*)

YUAN-YUAN: Comrades of the Liberation Army,
some reactionaries have escaped and I can't find my
classmate Tung Ah-nan!

CHEN: Give chase to the enemy, Eighth Squad Leader!
(*Goes to search the building.*)

CHAO: Yes.

YUAN-YUAN: I'm coming along too.

CHAO (*motioning for her to stay back*): Bullets don't
have eyes. I can't save you if you are hit. (*Stamping his
foot*) Stay back! (*Exit.*)

CHEN (*comes out of the building*): Come back! Hey
you, come back!
(*LIN YUAN-YUAN runs off into the distance. Off-
stage LU TA-CHENG calls: "Third Platoon Leader,
Chen Hsi!" Underground Party member CHOU TEH-
KUEI comes in with Company Commander LU TA-
CHENG and Political Instructor LU HUA.*)

LU TA-CHENG: Have you caught them?

CHEN: No. They've fled!

LU TA-CHENG: So the bandits want to fight guerrilla
warfare with us right here on the Nanking Road, eh?
(*Takes out his Mauser.*) Watch me bring them back
alive, Uncle Chou. (*Exit.*)

LU HUA: Where are those students?

7

CHEN: That girl left with the Eighth Squad Leader. I can't find Tung Ah-nan.

CHOU: Can't find him? Let's go. Quick!

LU HUA: Uncle Chou, the underground Party here has done a good job. Leading the workers and students, you protected the factories and schools and welcomed the Liberation Army into Shanghai, and now you're helping us to ferret out the bandits. You've done a great deal of work. Take a rest.

CHOU: What? Do you think because I'm old I'm useless? Comrade, I'm still as much a soldier now as I was twenty-five years ago when I fought and charged the British on this same street. But let's get down to business. (*Motioning*) Follow me!

LU HUA (*to CHEN HSI*): Let's go!

(*A MESSENGER enters.*)

MESSENGER: Reporting! An urgent order!

LU HUA (*taking the order*): Go quickly and fetch back the Company Commander.

(*The MESSENGER runs out.*)

(*CHAO TA-TA enters at a trot.*)

CHAO: Reporting! I met a woman. She was afraid of me at first, but then she asked me about a suitcase. Said someone had taken it from her.

LU HUA (*surprised*): What suitcase? Who took it? Ask her to come here. (*CHAO TA-TA yells at the woman.*) Don't shout so rudely! You'll frighten these Shanghai people.

CHAO: Very good. (*In a soft gentle voice*) Hey, don't be afraid. Please come here; our Instructor wants to see you. Come here!

8

(Stupefied with terror, MRS. LIN comes towards him. When she sees the squad of Liberation Army soldiers standing before her, she hastily turns to run.)

CHAO: Come back! What are you afraid of? We're Liberation Army men!

MRS. LIN: I'm not afraid. Don't bother — it was just a suitcase.

LU HUA: What kind of suitcase?

MRS. LIN *(making a gesture)*: So big. It had ... it had a little. ...

LU HUA: What sort of person took it? What was he wearing? What did he look like?

CHAO: Speak up! Was he wearing a uniform like mine?

MRS. LIN *(nodding)*: Yes. He said he was a Liberation Army man.

CHAO: A soldier in the Liberation Army took it? You —
(MRS. LIN winces.)

LU HUA: Don't go away! We must get to the bottom of this.

MRS. LIN *(horrified)*: Just forget about it. It's hard for a soldier not to take a little something. But if one of you officers happen to find that suitcase, please notify me. *(Opening her purse, she draws out a stack of banknotes and holds them out to the Political Instructor.)* Here, take this small token. You boys can buy a drink with it. *(Seeing the Political Instructor smile, she takes out two gold bars.)* Take this as my gift to you brave fighters.

LU HUA: Take back your money. I'd like you to know that we're Liberation Army men; we're Chairman Mao's soldiers. We've never so much as taken a piece of thread from the people!

9

MRS. LIN: Don't be ashamed. I've seen many soldiers in Shanghai — British, American, Japanese and Kuomintang. What difference does it make if you accept a little money!

CHAO (*angrily*): Go away! (*MRS. LIN draws back in fright.*) What do you think Liberation Army men are? (*Frightened, MRS. LIN goes away.*)

LU HUA: Now look what you've done, Chao Ta-ta!

CHAO: What kind of behaviour is this?

LU HUA: That's their way of doing things.

CHEN: It's just like seeing a ghost in broad daylight.

LU HUA: Since you're here, you must learn to be patient.

CHEN: I think she was deliberately trying to ruin the reputation of the Liberation Army!

CHAO: I'm going to drag her back!

LU HUA: Don't act so rashly! We'll spoil everything if we act before investigating. Didn't you study the Rules for Soldiers Entering the City before we came here? (*The MESSENGER comes in with LU TA-CHENG and CHOU TEH-KUEI.*)

LU TA-CHENG: What's up, Instructor?

LU HUA: We have a new task!

LU TA-CHENG: That's fine. I've just begun to long for the front again now that Shanghai's been liberated. Are we to go to the Choushan Islands or Taiwan?

LU HUA: No, the Nanking Road!

LU TA-CHENG: What does this mean? (*As he reads the order the colour drains from his face.*) What? We're being based in a street?

LU HUA: That's the idea! We're to stand guard here and defend Shanghai.

10

CHOU (*stepping forward to shake the company com-mander's hand*): That's just fine! We welcome you!

LU TA-CHENG: Uncle Chou! Fighting battles is our job. This is the first time our Army has been asked to keep watch on a street.

CHEN: That's fine! We're the men who liberated Shanghai. It's only right we should walk up and down the streets for a while. We'll see what sort of a place Shanghai is!

LU TA-CHENG: No more of your silly talk! (*Holding up the order*) Do you think the order means sightseeing in Shanghai?
(*FIGHTER A enters running.*)

FIGHTER A: We have found a young student in the gutter!

LU HUA: Where is he?

FIGHTER A: He's being brought here.
(*AH-NAN is brought in on a stretcher. LIN YUAN-YUAN follows.*)

CHOU (*stepping up to the stretcher*): Ah-nan! Ah-nan!

AH-NAN (*coming to*): Uncle Chou!... That bandit, Director Ma . . . beat me up. . . . Now he's called. . . . (*Loses consciousness.*)

LU HUA: Hurry, take him to the hospital!
(*FIGHTERS A and B carry AH-NAN out. LIN YUAN-YUAN follows them.*)

CHOU: Company Commander! Political Instructor! That Director Ma is the same villain who killed Ah-nan's father right here on the Nanking Road. Now he's gone underground.

LU HUA: Comrades, it seems that standing guard here on the Nanking Road is not going to be so easy. We've won the victory, but now we're faced with a new task in the class struggle!

LU TA-CHENG: As long as we have the leadership of the Party and the support of the working class, I don't mind. Let's go!

CHAO: Where are we going?

LU TA-CHENG: Just like me, you have no brains! We're going to keep watch on a street!

(*They go off in the morning sun towards the beat of drums which is welcoming them.*)

(*The stage darkens for a change of scene.*)

SCENE TWO

The Nanking Road. Lamp-lighting time.

Changing neon signs on a skyscraper in the background blaze with advertisements for the opera "The White-Haired Girl" and the Hollywood film "Bathing Beauty". The beat of drums is heard near the entrance to the Park, where a celebration is to be held.

Songs from the Liberated Areas alternate with jazz music.

AH-JUNG cries out "Evening paper!", AH-HSIANG shouts "Buy tuberoses!" and FEIFEI is selling the magazine "Hollywood Screen" and tickets for films. They weave their way through the throngs of well-dressed people.

AH-JUNG: Buy an evening paper! Read how the Yankees were defeated at Wusung, how the old society changes man into a ghost and how the new society changes a ghost into man! Buy the evening paper! We welcome you to the celebration in the Park! See the Liberation Army men perform the play *The White-Haired Girl* and other special features!

FEIFEI (*in the shadow of a building*): Buy a ticket for the film *Bathing Beauty*! Buy *Hollywood Screen* and pictures of Hollywood stars. Tickets to the night clubs — two for the price of one! (*Seeing AH-JUNG, FEIFEI beckons to the boy with his fore-finger.*) Evening paper! (*AH-JUNG moves towards him.*)   How much do the Communists pay you?

(*AH-JUNG ignores him.*)

FEIFEI (*blocking his path*):   I'll buy the whole lot.

AH-JUNG: Get out of the way!

FEIFEI: See this! (*Patting his bulging pocket*) That's money!

AH-JUNG (*pushing him aside*):   Give it to the devil. (*Goes away.*)

FEIFEI: I want an evening paper! I want news from Hollywood!

AH-JUNG: Listen! (*Shouting*)   Read how the Yankees were defeated. See the Liberation Army men perform *The White-Haired Girl* and other special features of the celebration in the Park. . . .

(*FEIFEI clenches his fists, annoyed. AH-JUNG goes out, shouting.*)

(*OLD SEVEN runs in.*)

OLD SEVEN: What bad luck, Feifei! The Liberation Army men are guarding the entrance to the Park! It's difficult to sneak in!

FEIFEI: You just watch me!

OLD SEVEN: Don't! Someone who knows us is standing guard there. I never thought that little bastard we beat up and threw in the gutter would join the Liberation Army and stand guard at the entrance. Look, he's coming this way!

FEIFEI (*starting towards the entrance*):   Let me have a try at it, Brother!

OLD SEVEN (*grabbing hold of him*):   Hold on a minute. I'm going back to talk this over with Old K. We've got to get rid of that little bastard tonight, or else —

(*Dressed in a Liberation Army man's uniform, AH-NAN runs after OLD SEVEN who takes to his heels.*)

FEIFEI (*smiling and moving forward*): I salute you, comrade of the Liberation Army. You've done a good job of driving away the foreign aggressors and wiping out the reactionaries. You've helped the Shanghai people to get their own back. Have a cigarette.

(*AH-NAN pushes his hand aside.*)

FEIFEI (*stepping forward*): Please accept these with my compliments! (*Holding out two movie tickets*) They're for a picture from Hollywood. Everything's on me. Here's a picture of a film star, too. (*Waving the picture in front of AH-NAN's face*) There's a song on the back. (*Shuffling around he sings a rowdy song.*)

AH-NAN: Ah, that's just fine! You come with me! (*Grabs hold of his arm.*)

FEIFEI: What's the matter? Aren't we good friends?

AH-NAN: Who sent you out to distribute these leaflets? (*Holds up the leaflet.*)

FEIFEI: What! A leaflet? (*Reading*) "Please be on guard against brain-washing and poisoning at the Park." My goodness! I know nothing about it.

AH-NAN: Who were you talking to just now? That man wearing a cap?

FEIFEI: Was it a man or a woman, young or old?

AH-NAN: Don't play the fool with me! I'm no greenhorn. Let's go! You're working hand in glove with him.

FEIFEI: Spare my life, Comrade! It's not me you want, it's him. (*Pointing*) Look, over there!

(*When AH-NAN turns to look, FEIFEI wrenches himself free and runs away.*)

(*CHAO TA-TA enters.*)

CHAO: Tung Ah-nan!

AH-NAN: Here! Just a minute, Squad Leader, I'm going to catch a hooligan at the dance-hall on the opposite side of the street!

CHAO (*astonished*): What? Going to a dance-hall to catch a hooligan? Come back here, you wastrel!

(*Just as CHAO TA-TA is about to give chase, he comes face to face with two nuns. They stop immediately upon seeing CHAO TA-TA. Their dress amazes CHAO TA-TA. He fondles the butt of his Sten-gun. Upon seeing this, the nuns turn pale and hasten on their way. CHAO TA-TA heaves a sigh of relief. The nuns pass on behind him, making the sign of the cross.*

A WELL-DRESSED WOMAN and her husband pass by. She is carrying many parcels, large and small. When she sees CHAO TA-TA, she turns to speak to her husband.)

WOMAN: See! How dark-skinned that soldier is! Teehee.... (*Gives CHAO TA-TA a black teddy-bear and inadvertently drops her purse.*)

CHAO: Come back! (*Returns the teddy-bear and waves her on.*) Now, go away!

WOMAN: My, this soldier is rough! (*Goes off with her husband.*)

(*When CHAO TA-TA turns round he sees the purse and picks it up.*)

CHAO: Hey!

(*"Buy tuberoses! Buy a tuberose!" AH-HSIANG, a young flower girl with two long plaits, comes up to CHAO TA-TA and stands in his way.*)

AH-HSIANG: Won't you buy a tuberose? (*CHAO TA-TA tries to keep clear of her.*) Oh, do buy a flower

16

from me! (*CHAO TA-TA turns his back to her.*) These flowers are fragrant. You see, I have roses, gardenias, and jasmine! Please take your pick; they're all very fragrant. If you don't believe me, take one home and put it by your pillow, I guarantee that it'll scent your room all night. Your wife'll certainly like it!

CHAO (*at a loss*): Will you please stand aside, Miss!

AH-HSIANG: I won't charge you anything to smell one. (*Holds a flower up to CHAO TA-TA's nose.*)

CHAO: Get out of the way! (*Covering his nose*) I've lost my sense of smell; got a cold.

AH-HSIANG: Ah! Comrade soldier, be kind enough to buy a flower. You'll be saving me from hunger and a beating. You don't know the sufferings of a flower girl. I borrowed the money at exorbitant interest to start up in business. Today is the deadline for me to pay back my debt. My mother's at home waiting for me to come back so that we can have a meal. Have pity on me.

(*CHAO TA-TA is moved.*)

AH-HSIANG: Please buy one! (*Goes up and sticks a flower in the pocket of CHAO TA-TA's uniform.*)
(*At this moment there is the flare of a flashbulb and the click of a shutter. An American reporter enters carrying a camera. He acts as though quite unconcerned. There is another flash. The reporter says "Thank you" and goes on his way.*)
(*Off-stage: "Catch him! Catch him!"*)

CHAO: Come back here! Don't try to run away! (*Begins to give chase.*)
(*AH-JUNG enters chasing after the American reporter.*)

17

AH-JUNG (*to CHAO TA-TA*): He's taken pictures in a prohibited area. (*Goes after the American reporter.*)

(*Pretending to be drunk, FEIFEI staggers up and collides with CHAO TA-TA. CHAO TA-TA pushes FEIFEI aside and he falls to the ground.*)

CHAO (*helping FEIFEI up while shouting*): Catch him, catch him! (*Hardly has CHAO TA-TA released FEIFEI than he reels and falls on CHAO TA-TA again.*)

(*AH-NAN comes in running.*)

AH-NAN: What's up, Squad Leader?

CHAO: Hurry! Catch that American reporter and seize his camera.

AH-NAN (*pointing at FEIFEI*): He's the hooligan, Squad Leader!

CHAO (*pointing at the American reporter*): Hurry up, catch him.

AH-NAN: Yes! Hey you! (*Chases after the American reporter.*)

CHAO (*puzzled*): Who are you? A hooligan?

FEIFEI: My name's Feifei. I'm a docker.

CHAO: A docker? (*Sympathetically*) Hey, pedicab!

FEIFEI: Thanks! Had a few sips to celebrate our liberation. You're really ... (*Singing*) "The sky in the Liberated Areas is bright. ..."

(*A pedicab driver enters.*)

CHAO: Hurry, take this man home!

FEIFEI: See you again.

(*FEIFEI snaps to attention, throws a kiss at CHAO TA-TA and says "Bye-bye!" The pedicab driver takes FEIFEI away.*)

(*AH-NAN and AH-JUNG prod the American reporter along. A knot of people crowd around them to
watch the excitement.*)

AH-NAN: Get moving, Mr. Reporter! What have
you been doing on the sly? (*To CHAO TA-TA*) Is
this the one, Squad Leader?

CHAO: That's him! (*To the American reporter*) Give
me that camera!

REPORTER: What right have you to demand the
camera of a foreign reporter? Don't you know that's
a violation of international law?

AH-NAN: Violation of international law? Do you
know what era and place this is? You still take
Shanghai to be a paradise for adventurers like you!
There's military control here now! You're taking
pictures of our guard posts, and attempting to break up
our celebration in the Park. You've violated our law!
(*Commotion in the crowd.*)

REPORTER: What celebration in the Park! What a
joke! I want everyone here to know that this is only a
trick! It's political propaganda and brain-washing....

CHAO: That's enough!

REPORTER: Where's your democracy, your freedom?
Why, you are even taking away a man's right to speak.

CHAO: You have no freedom to spread reactionary
propaganda!

AH-NAN: Give me that camera, or I shall stop being
polite. (*Brings his Sten-gun to the ready.*)

REPORTER (*flabbergasted*): What! You'd shoot? Re-
sorting to force, eh? Have you laid aside your
Eight-Point Covenant? I would like everyone here
to speak up for my rights! I would like to hear the
voice of real freedom here on the Nanking Road!

19

(*A MAN WEARING GLASSES draws CHAO TA-TA aside and whispers.*)

MAN WEARING GLASSES: Don't start trouble! You shouldn't rile the Americans. You've just liberated Shanghai and haven't settled down yet. It'll be very difficult to straighten things out if you make a big issue out of this.

ICE-CREAM VENDOR (*wearing a T shirt bearing the trade mark of "Belle" ice-cream*): Hey you, my friend wearing glasses! If you don't have the courage to do something good, don't try to persuade others to do something bad. Keep up your courage! If the sky falls down the Liberation Army will hold it up.

CROWD: And it has the support of the Shanghai people.

CAPITALIST (*nervously*): Don't cause trouble. We've still got to trade with the Americans. If we don't trade with them, where shall we Shanghai people get our food?

DANCE-HALL HOSTESS: Very true! How can we live without the Americans?

ICE-CREAM VENDOR (*to the CAPITALIST*): You don't have to worry. If there's a famine, it'll never come knocking on your door.

CAPITALIST: I'm worried for everyone, because if we continue to make trouble, Shanghai will fall.

(*CHOU TEH-KUEI emerges from the crowd, with a bag of tools slung across his shoulder.*)

CHOU: What's all this about Shanghai falling?

AH-NAN: Uncle Chou!

CHOU (*stepping towards the MAN WEARING GLASSES*): This man appears to have good intentions. (*To the CAPITALIST*) And you're a boss, I

20

suppose? Though we have different backgrounds we're all Chinese and drink water from the same Huangpu River. Then why do you help the foreigners and attack your fellow countrymen? For more than a hundred years now, we here in Shanghai have been bullied and forced by foreigners to work like dogs. Right? But now we're liberated. Right? We've stood up. Right? Then let's stop talking like slaves. Let's stick our chests out and look like real Chinese. If we unite, Shanghai will never fall. "Yankees, go home!"

(*The crowd repeat the slogan.*)

AH-NAN (*starting singing and directing the song*): "Unity is strength. . . ."

(*The AMERICAN REPORTER is surrounded by singing people.*)

CHOU (*stepping towards the AMERICAN REPORTER*): Listen to the voice of freedom on the Nanking Road, Mr. Reporter!

(*The AMERICAN REPORTER is at a loss. The sound of singing comes at him from all directions. He is forced to raise both hands and walk over to CHAO TA-TA and TUNG AH-NAN.*)

REPORTER: Will you please maintain order! (*Handing over his camera*) It's quite possible for us to solve things peacefully.

CHAO: Let's go to the office of the Committee of Military Control.

REPORTER: I'm not interested in going there.

(*The singing starts again.*)

REPORTER: Let's go!

CHAO: Where?

REPORTER: To the office of the Committee of Military Control.

AH-NAN (*to CHAO TA-TA*): Where's that hooligan?

CHAO: I sent him home in a pedicab.

AH-NAN: Aiya! He's working in league with the American reporter!

CHAO: Really? Hm! You take care of the post, I'll be right back! (*Goes off with the AMERICAN REPORTER.*)

REPORTER (*turning round as he leaves*): Don't feel so proud, Mr. Liberation Army man. You've come here red; but in three months' time you're going to meet your fate right here on the Nanking Road.

(*Helplessly, the AMERICAN REPORTER leaves amid laughter.*)

ICE-CREAM VENDOR: Hey Yankee, here's an ice-lolly[1] for you! (*Flings an ice-lolly at him.*)

CHOU: Come, friends! Let's go in; the celebration in the Park is about to start!

(*The crowd streams towards the entrance to the Park.*)

AH-NAN (*moving forward*): You spoke well just now, Uncle Chou.

CHOU: We must keep on our toes, Ah-nan. The enemy is trying for all he's worth to destroy our celebration in the Park. We must let him know who we are.

AH-NAN: Right! Won't you come to our company headquarters for a while!

CHOU: I can't. The power plant has sent me here on duty; they're afraid that something may go wrong with the lights. See you later. (*Exit.*)

---

[1] Ice-lolly: A sweet flavoured piece of ice.

AH-NAN: So long!

MAN WEARING GLASSES (*mopping the sweat from his brow, goes up and taps AH-NAN on the shoulder*): What you just did is very dangerous, Little Soldier!

HIS WIFE: Are we still going to the Park?

MAN WEARING GLASSES: Well, it's a matter of formality — to keep the Communists in a good mood. (*Exeunt*).

CAPITALIST: There's something in what that American said.

WIFE OF CAPITALIST: I heard that *The White-Haired Girl* is really a frightful sight — a living ghost! Let's go and see the *Bathing Beauty*.

CAPITALIST: Right! Otherwise we'll have hell to pay when the Americans return. Let's go back.

AH-NAN: Hey you! What kind of talk is that?

CAPITALIST: I'm sorry. You go your way and I'll go mine, and we'll never meet again. (*Goes off with his wife.*)

AH-NAN: I can see the ghost of American imperialism clinging to you.

(*Carrying a waist-drum, CHU MAN-LI enters hand in hand with LO KE-WEN. They are looking for LIN YUAN-YUAN.*)

LO: Where did you say Yuan-yuan was, Man-li?

CHU: Let's go. She was beating the waist-drum with me just now.

LO: Good heavens! She was playing that thing?

CHU: She's also going to take part in the performance of *The White-Haired Girl*.

LO: Hurry, let's find her! (*Taking a wooden comb from his pocket to comb his hair, he carelessly drops his tickets to the Park performance.*)

AH-NAN: Hey, you've dropped your tickets. (*Picks them up.*)

LO: I'm sorry. I've lost all interest in it. . . . Oh, so it's you. . . . Hey! (*Shaking his head*) I never thought you'd join the army. What a pity! (*Turns to go.*)

AH-NAN: Come back!

LO (*instinctively raising both arms*): You, you. . . . (*Drops his arms to his side.*)

AH-NAN: Here, take them back!

CHU (*takes the tickets and turns to LO KE-WEN*): You're really backward in your thinking. Let's go! (*Leads him out.*)

(*LIN YUAN-YUAN enters from the side with a waist-drum slung on her arm. Seeing AH-NAN, she sneaks behind him and snatches the evening paper out of his hand.*)

AH-NAN (*turning round*): Yuan-yuan!

YUAN-YUAN (*shaking his hand warmly*): I never knew you'd joined the Liberation Army! Let's have a good look at you! How smart you look!

AH-NAN: Don't act like this in public, Yuan-yuan!

YUAN-YUAN (*smiling*): Tell me why didn't you write to me after you left the hospital. I've been inquiring about you everywhere.

AH-NAN: I've been inquiring about you too. I thought that as you'd become a great performer with your name in all the papers you wouldn't recognize me any more.

YUAN-YUAN: Stop making fun of me. (*Lowering her head*) I'm acting and singing a very small role in the opera *The White-Haired Girl.*

AH-NAN: Didn't the paper say you had been specially invited to sing a solo at the celebration in the Park?

24

YUAN-YUAN: Yes, during the closing ceremony. Anyway, there's nothing grand about it.

AH-NAN: But I think you are grand. The performance of your troupe is an important event; even the Liberation Army men are doing everything to help you.

YUAN-YUAN: Is that so?

AH-NAN: Yes, of course!

YUAN-YUAN: Will you come and see our performance? The première is tonight. I hear that the mayor will be present! I'm very excited. Won't you come, Ah-nan? (*Seeing him hesitate*) I'll give a better performance if you're there.

AH-NAN: I'd like to go but I'm not free.

YUAN-YUAN: What's detaining you?

AH-NAN: I'll have to stand guard at the Park.

YUAN-YUAN: But our performance will be given in the Park. What's wrong with going to see a play? Come on, let's go! (*Catches him by the arm.*)

(*LO KE-WEN comes towards them. CHU MAN-LI steals away.*)

LO: Yuan-yuan!

YUAN-YUAN: Cousin!

(*A pause.*)

LO: Come back with me, Yuan-yuan! Do listen to me, Yuan-yuan! Aunt is waiting for you!

YUAN-YUAN: Wait till my performance is over.

LO: I'm against your taking part in such a performance. That's not a real opera but plain foolishness!

YUAN-YUAN (*anxiously*): Don't say any more, Cousin!

LO: I'm going to speak out. It's nothing but political propaganda, hocus-pocus . . . and. . . .

AH-NAN (*loudly*): Shut up! Don't be a mouthpiece of the American imperialists!

LO: What? You . . . I don't want to argue with you! (*Tugging at LIN YUAN-YUAN's arm*) Come to your senses, Yuan-yuan! Don't be their stool-pigeon; if you do you're done for! (*Pulls her away.*)

AH-NAN: What are you trying to do? Break up our celebration in the Park? You'd better be careful. Don't fall for the enemy's tricks.

(*LIN YUAN-YUAN wrenches herself free and seeks cover behind AH-NAN.*)

LO: What? You're on his side. (*Buries his head in his hands.*) I'll tell your mother. (*Storms out.*)

YUAN-YUAN: Wait a minute, Cousin! Come back. . . . (*Excitedly*) What shall I do, Ah-nan?

AH-NAN (*stolidly*): Stand up for your rights and take part in the celebration.

YUAN-YUAN: Then come with me. I haven't had supper yet.

AH-NAN: All right.

(*CHEN HSI enters.*)

AH-NAN: Reporting! Platoon Leader, can I have leave? I have an appointment with a schoolmate of mine.

CHEN: Who is he?

YUAN-YUAN: How do you do, Platoon Leader? (*Bows.*)

CHEN: Ah! We've met before!

AH-NAN: Platoon Leader, it's her. . . . (*Lacks the courage to continue.*)

YUAN-YUAN (*nodding*): I . . . I think. . . .

CHEN: What's the matter? Go ahead and say whatever you have on your mind.

YUAN-YUAN: I'd like Ah-nan to come and have supper with me and then go to the performance in the

26

Park afterwards. Will you give him permission, Platoon Leader?

CHEN (*to AH-NAN*): What do you think?

(*AH-NAN throws a glance at LIN YUAN-YUAN.*)

YUAN-YUAN: Please give him permission. I'll be very happy if you do.

CHEN: So it seems I can only agree!

YUAN-YUAN (*jumping up and down*): Oh, you're really wonderful! (*Shakes his hand.*)

CHEN (*beckoning for AH-NAN to come*): Come here! Put your cap on straight and button up your tunic. You're in the Liberation Army; you must look dignified, or you'll make yourself the laughing-stock of the Shanghai people. Do you need any money?

YUAN-YUAN: No, he doesn't.

CHEN: Watch your behaviour!

AH-NAN: Yes!

YUAN-YUAN: Thank you, Platoon Leader! (*Goes out with AH-NAN.*)

(*CHU MAN-LI watches them go. Unexpectedly, she runs into CHEN HSI.*)

CHU (*quickly coping with the situation*): Hello, Platoon Leader Chen! (*Shaking his hand warmly*) Don't you recognize me? I'm a student of the Chunghua School. I did some propaganda work with you during the celebration of July 1.[1] Have you forgotten that you came to our school to make a report and tell some stories?

CHEN: Oh! I remember now. But it's a pity I've forgotten your name.

CHU: My name's Chu Man-li. Do you have an address book?

---

[1] Birthday of the Chinese Communist Party.

27

CHEN: Yes. (*Tugging at his pocket to extract the address book, he shakes the three medals on his chest.*)

CHU: How beautiful they are!

(*CHEN HSI smiles and hands her the address book. CHU MAN-LI writes her name in it.*)

CHU: We're having a dance with the Liberation Army men at the celebration in the Park tonight. Are you coming?

CHEN: I don't dance.

CHU: You can take your choice of dancing, singing, watching performances or listening to story-telling. Your stories about heroes are very moving and educational. We'd like you to tell us some more stories.

(*CHEN HSI smiles.*)

CHU: Do come. It's going to be exciting. Some film stars are going to be present!

CHEN: Really?

CHU: Uh-huh. They'll like to hear your stories about heroes.

CHEN: All right, I'll come.

CHU: I'll be waiting for you at the entrance. (*Waves him good-bye.*) See you later! (*Exit.*)

CHEN: So long. (*He waves after her.*)

(*MESSENGER enters.*)

MESSENGER: Third Platoon Leader! Someone's here to see you!

CHEN: Who?

MESSENGER: Chun-ni. (*Beckoning*) Old Mess Officer!

CHEN: What are you shouting for? Tell her I'm not here. Send her to Company Headquarters.

MESSENGER (*grabbing hold of him*): What did you say? You mean you don't want to see your wife! Fancy

28

being so bashful. (*Shouting*) Old Mess Officer, the Third Platoon Leader says that he's not here!

CHEN: What are you trying to do?

(*HUNG MAN-TANG, known as the Old Mess Officer, enters with CHUN-NI, carrying vegetables in baskets suspended from a carrying-pole. CHUN-NI has the carrying-pole which she uses to take grain to the front. She also has a bundle wrapped in red cloth.*)

HUNG: Look who's here, Chen Hsi! Now just look how red in the face you two are. (*Tugging at CHEN HSI's sleeve*) Go over and speak to her.

CHEN: We should be more formal out here on the Nanking Road.

HUNG: Oho! You're really taking your work seriously, eh?

CHEN: It's only right that I do. Look how many pairs of eyes are watching us.

HUNG: Hurry, go over and speak to her!

CHEN (*stepping towards CHUN-NI*): I salute you. (*The MESSENGER sniggers.*) What are you sniggering about?! (*To CHUN-NI*) What have you come for?
(*CHUN-NI lowers her head.*)

HUNG: Nonsense! Do you have to ask her why she's come? She's come to see you.
(*CHUN-NI smiles bashfully.*)

CHEN (*anxiously*): Stop shouting! Watch your behaviour! (*Moves closer to CHUN-NI.*) Why did you bring the carrying-pole? Swaying and bobbing up and down the streets. Suppose you strike someone with it!

HUNG: What are you saying? She's a model peasant in her support of the front. She also has a share in the liberation of Shanghai. Now she's come to see you with

29

the carrying-pole still in her hand. How thoughtful she is!

CHUN-NI: Don't say any more, Uncle.

CHEN: So, you've been working hard!

HUNG: You're talking nonsense. Hurry up and show your wife around this big city of Shanghai.

CHEN: I'm busy, I'm in charge of the squad on duty.

HUNG: I give you leave.

CHUN-NI: He's very busy. Don't hold up his work.

HUNG: Do you mean to say I'm the one who's wrong?

CHUN-NI: Let's drop it, Uncle.

CHEN: Don't embarrass me, Old Mess Officer.

HUNG: So, there's nothing doing! I've done everything to bring you two together, but I was wrong to do it.

CHUN-NI: Don't be angry, Uncle.

CHEN: I salute you, all right? (*Escorts them out.*) (*AH-HSIANG runs in, shouting: "Ah-nan! ... Ah-nan!" When she sees that AH-NAN isn't there she goes off towards the Park entrance. CHAO TA-TA enters. AH-HSIANG hurries back from the Park entrance.*)

AH-HSIANG (*seeing CHAO TA-TA*): Hey Liberation Army man, please tell me where Ah-nan is. I have something very important to talk over with him. Where is he?

CHAO: Who are you?

AH-HSIANG: I'm his sister.

CHAO: He's standing guard at the entrance to the Park.

AH-HSIANG: He's not there.

CHAO: Not there? (*Looks around.*)

AH-HSIANG (*looking around and seeing OLD SEVEN coming after her*): Liberation Army man! (*Suddenly*

kneels down before CHAO TA-TA.) Please save me!
Save me!

CHAO: Please get up. Tell me what is the matter.

AH-HSIANG: The dead-line to pay my debt is today.
That man's chasing me and is going to beat me again.

CHAO *(spotting blood at the corner of her mouth, he
quickly helps her to stand up)*: Stand up! No one will
dare touch you when I'm around!

(OLD SEVEN enters, dressed in civilian clothes.)

OLD SEVEN: Hello, Comrade of the Liberation Army.
Please forgive me, but this is a family affair.

CHAO: Your family affair! What's she to you?

OLD SEVEN: She's the adopted daughter of my boss.
(Pretending to be kind to AH-HSIANG) Come here,
Ah-hsiang! You must be hungry! Come, I'll take you
to the boss. He's waiting for you to have dinner with
him at the hotel.

AH-HSIANG: I'm not hungry. *(Cowers in fear.)*

OLD SEVEN: Don't be afraid. Come here. I'll put
in a word for you to the boss and pay off your debt,
too. Come here. *(AH-HSIANG moves towards him.
OLD SEVEN takes out a handful of banknotes and
thrusts them into AH-HSIANG's hand.)* Our boss
knows your family is having a hard time. Take this
money and buy yourself something. If you find that
man for us, we'll forget about the debt.

AH-HSIANG: No, no. . . .

*(OLD SEVEN knocks AH-HSIANG down, and then
proceeds to beat her.)*

CHAO: Stop! *(Pushes OLD SEVEN aside.)* If you
hit her again, I'll kill you!

31

OLD SEVEN: All right. All right! I'll let you off now for this officer's sake. But you know what's in store for you! (*Bustles off.*)

CHAO: Come here, Little Sister. (*Gives her a handkerchief to wipe the blood off the corner of her mouth.*) What is the relation between that man and you? Why does he treat you so cruelly?

(*AH-HSIANG bursts into tears.*)

CHAO: Tell me!

AH-HSIANG: I can't. I could never tell you all in a few words. . . .

CHAO: Tell me! I'll avenge you as though I were your brother.

AH-HSIANG (*shaking her head*): I don't want you to be involved in this, Comrade. (*Prepares to leave.*)

CHAO: Where are you going?

AH-HSIANG: To look for my brother — er — going back home.

CHAO: Wait! (*Taking out his purse and thrusts it into her hand*) Take this money.

AH-HSIANG: I can't take your money.

CHAO: Take it!

AH-HSIANG: This. . . . (*Attempts to kneel.*)

CHAO: Now go!

(*CHAO TA-TA watches AH-HSIANG as she slowly walks away. The voice of Hsi Erh, heroine in the play "The White-Haired Girl", is heard singing softly. "The north wind blows; the snow twirls...." CHAO TA-TA walks along very depressed. CHEN HSI enters.*)

CHAO: Have you seen Ah-nan?

CHEN: He went to have a meal with a girl classmate of his.

CHAO: What? How can he do that? He must be put into solitary confinement! (*Starts to leave.*)

CHEN: Come back. Can't you keep your voice down in the streets! It's me who gave him permission to go.

CHAO: How can you do that, Platoon Leader?

CHEN: You are short of brains. You big blusterer! Don't you know that one must be flexible and make allowances when leading soldiers from Shanghai. The big-stick policy won't do.

CHAO: I still have something to say about that!

CHEN: Tell me when you come back.

CHAO: Very good! I'll go and see how things are going in my squad.

CHEN: There's no need. Now, now stand aside. You dark-skinned peasant.

(*CHAO TA-TA turns and leaves. When he sees the Company Commander and the Political Instructor coming, he salutes them and goes off looking very depressed.*)

LU TA-CHENG (*watches CHAO TA-TA going away*): What's the matter, Chen Hsi?

CHEN: Here! (*Snaps to attention.*)

LU TA-CHENG: How are things here?

CHEN: Everything's quiet and normal.

LU TA-CHENG: You seem to think all is peaceful and calm on the Nanking Road.

CHEN: Even the breeze is fragrant.

LU TA-CHENG (*astounded*): What did you say?

CHEN (*muttering*): The breeze is fragrant. . . . (*Goes off.*)

LU TA-CHENG: You, you. . . .

LU HUA (*to himself*): Even the breeze is fragrant, eh?

LU TA-CHENG: What rubbish!

33

LU HUA: Yes, Old K is dangerous but the fragrant breeze is even worse.

LU TA-CHENG: If we don't get things straightened out, we'll never be able to hold our own here.

(*Jazz music fills the air. Dazzling neon lights flicker on and off.*)

(*The stage darkens for a change of scene.*)

SCENE THREE

The same night as in Scene Two.

At company headquarters. All is quiet in the courtyard.

There is music in the distance.

In the background there are tall buildings with neon lights blinking faintly.

CHAO TA-TA whose brain is pounding with the monotonous beat of music is in bed with his head under the quilt, trying to sleep. LU HUA enters carrying an electric torch. He flashes it on to CHAO TA-TA's bed. LU TA-CHENG follows him in.

LU HUA: Who's that? Is that you, Ta-ta?
  (*CHAO TA-TA doesn't answer.*)

LU HUA: Sleeping with your shoes on and not covered properly. (*Takes CHAO TA-TA's shoes off and stretches the quilt.*)

CHAO (*sitting up suddenly*): I can't sleep, Instructor!

LU HUA (*switching on the lights*): What's wrong with you? (*Feels his forehead.*) Not feeling well? Your hands are a bit cold. Are you ill? I'll fetch a doctor.

CHAO (*excitedly*): Instructor.... I can't take any more of this.

LU HUA: What's the matter, Ta-ta? Has something gone wrong? Tell me!

35

CHAO: Send me to the front, some place where there's fighting. I don't want to stay here on the Nanking Road.

LU HUA: Why?

CHAO (*resentfully*): I have a dark skin!

LU TA-CHENG (*a smile flits across his face, then speaking seriously*): A dark skin? You can't stand guard and be the master of your country because you have a dark skin? What sort of problem is this? (*Goes over to the window and looks out.*) How did your skin become dark? It shows that as a soldier you've been frequently exposed to the sun and that you're healthy. It's an honour and not a shame. (*Exit.*)

LU HUA: You always did well on the battlefield, Ta-ta. Why are you so disheartened since you've come to Shanghai?

CHAO: I'm fed up! Look at those lights, listen to that music! Everything here is topsyturvy! I don't mind if the bourgeoisie say I'm dark-skinned; I can work for the revolution just the same. If they can't get used to me I can't get used to them either. If it weren't for dark faces like mine there wouldn't be any liberation. But when my leader calls me a "dark-skinned peasant".

LU HUA: Who called you that?

CHAO: My platoon leader. He said I was a big blusterer and that I didn't know how to deal with Tung Ah-nan, that Shanghai soldier. When I said something against Ah-nan's going out with his girl friend just now, he criticized me by saying I had no brains.

LU HUA: H'm! No wonder Tung Ah-nan isn't back yet although it's so late. I suppose your platoon leader gave him permission to go.

36

CHAO (*nodding*): Company Headquarters put me in charge of the squad guarding the Park tonight; but my platoon leader told me he was going to take charge of things himself and said: "Stand aside, you dark-skinned peasant."

LU HUA: Didn't Company Headquarters give him leave? He isn't supposed to go away. Messenger!

(*The MESSENGER enters.*)

LU HUA: Have you arranged the room?

MESSENGER: The room has been cleared and cleaned.

LU HUA: Have you arranged a bed for them?

MESSENGER: Everything has been arranged. The Old Mess Officer put the bed there himself. Where are you going to stay, Instructor, now that you've let them have your room and bed?

LU HUA: Any place will do. Bring my bedding in here for tonight. How about me putting up with you tonight, Chao Ta-ta? (*CHAO TA-TA nods.*) All right then, (*to MESSENGER*) bring Chen Hsi's bedding to my room. When you've done that, go and look for Tung Ah-nan. If you see Chen Hsi tell him to come back and rest.

(*LU HUA and MESSENGER carry CHEN HSI's quilt and wash-basin away.*)

LU HUA: Just a minute, Chao Ta-ta, I'll be right back. (*Exit.*)

(*CHEN HSI enters humming a tune. He takes a pair of fancy socks out of his pocket and unwraps his leggings.*)

CHAO (*jumping up*): Stop singing, please! If you go on like that my head will burst!

37

CHEN (*smiling*): You're nothing but an old stick-in-the-mud! No wonder the Shanghai people are scared of you. (*Starts singing again.*)

CHAO (*exercising restraint*): Platoon Leader, I'd like to have a word with you.

CHEN: Some other time, eh?

CHAO: No! Now! I can't hold back any longer. I have some opinions about you!

CHEN: Since coming to Shanghai, you've had more to say than anyone. Nothing here pleases you! Why's that?

CHAO: You've to stay in the barracks and rest. I'm to take charge of the squad tonight. That's an order from the Political Instructor.

CHEN: That will never do! On such an occasion it's better you stand aside. Eh?

CHAO: What? (*Immediately starts to roll up his pack.*)

CHEN: Why are you rolling up your pack?

CHAO: I'm going to the front!

CHEN: Who's given you permission?

CHAO: I've already handed in my request to Company Headquarters.

(*Indifferently, CHEN HSI goes into the inner room.*)
(*There is a knock at the door.*)

CHEN (*from inner room*): Who's that? Go and see who's at the door, Chao Ta-ta!

(*CHAO TA-TA puts down his pack and goes to the door. He is amazed to see AH-HSIANG.*)

CHAO: Ah-hsiang!

AH-HSIANG: Is Ah-nan here?

CHAO: He hasn't come back yet.

AH-HSIANG: Then I must be running along.

38

CHAO: Why do you want to see him? Tell me. But if you don't want to, I'll get him to see you when he comes back.

AH-HSIANG: Tell him not to come home. Here, Comrade, take back your money.

CHAO: Why?

AH-HSIANG: I don't need it.

CHAO (*taking hold of her arm*): Tell me what's the matter?

CHEN (*from the inner room*): What's up, Chao Ta-ta?

AH-HSIANG: This is no place to talk. Can you come outside for a minute.

CHAO: You go first, I'll join you later.
(*AH-HSIANG leaves the courtyard. CHAO TA-TA goes back into the room, takes up his rifle and leaves. CHEN HSI comes out of the inner room carrying a pair of old cloth socks.*)

CHEN: Hey, so long! (*He throws the cloth socks out of the window.*)
(*HUNG MAN-TANG, who is just passing through the yard, picks up the socks and throws them back into the room.*)

CHEN (*seeing the socks*): Oh, so you're not willing to go, eh? All right then, stand aside. (*He kicks the socks into a corner, picks up a mirror and combs his hair.*)
(*CHUN-NI enters and put her hands over his eyes.*)

CHEN: Who's that? It must be Chun-ni. Let go! Let go! Please, don't do that. It'll be embarrassing if the comrades see us. Listen, someone's coming!
(*CHUN-NI snatches the comb out of his hand and keeps it out of his reach.*)

39

CHEN: Hurry, give it to me! You're a nuisance. You're trying to run away, eh? (*Chases after her.*)

CHUN-NI: Sit down and don't move.

(*CHEN HSI sits down against his will.*)

CHUN-NI (*stepping closer to him*): Chen Hsi, what day is today? I bet you've forgotten? Do you remember what we were doing on this day two years ago?

CHEN: Why do you ask that? I joined the militia and you joined the "support-the-front" supply team.

CHUN-NI: What else?

CHEN: I've forgotten.

CHUN-NI (*pushing his head back with her finger*): You deserve a good beating. Why did Aunt Hung bring you to my house?

CHEN (*as if just remembering*): Oh, that's right; we were married on this day two years ago.

CHUN-NI (*reflecting affectionately*): That night we sat facing each other without saying a word, but we were very happy. At daybreak on the third day I saw you off to join the army. My heart has been with you ever since. . . . But you haven't sent me one letter since you crossed the Yangtse. . . .

CHEN: I've been too busy.

CHUN-NI: No matter how busy you were you could have found time to write a letter if you'd wanted to. You could, at least, have sent a message by someone. I've been so worried about you. (*She sheds a few tears.*)

CHEN: Look at you. Don't let others see you acting like that!

CHUN-NI: I'm happy. Do you have to stand guard tonight?

CHEN: Yes, I must.

CHUN-NI: Can you take me along with you to have a look around?

CHEN: You? What would a man in the Liberation Army look like taking a woman with him?

CHUN-NI (*seeing some reason in what he says*): Don't be cross with me. Now that I'm with you, I don't want to leave you for one minute. All right, you go. I'll stay here and wait for you. Here, take these two eggs with you. You can eat them when you're hungry. (*She puts the eggs in the pocket of his new tunic.*)

CHEN (*tries to prevent her from doing so, but it is too late*): Look, you've soiled my tunic. (*Takes the eggs out of his pocket and puts them on the table.*)

CHUN-NI (*hurriedly wiping the stain off with her handkerchief*): See, now it's clean again.

CHEN (*smelling his fingers*): Damn it! My hand smells of them!
(*CHUN-NI uses her handkerchief to wipe his hand.*)

CHUN-NI: Ah! Don't be so particular. Is that all right? (*Giving him a handkerchief*) Take it with you.

CHEN: It's smelly anyhow! (*Throws the handkerchief to one side.*)

CHUN-NI: All right, I'm to blame! (*Looks askance at him.*)
(*Music starts in the Park; the celebration is beginning.*)

CHEN: Good gracious! (*Hurries to get ready.*)

CHUN-NI (*helping him to straighten his clothes; spots a tear on his sleeve*): Just look, you don't know how to take care of yourself when I'm not around. Come, let me mend it.

CHEN: Let go. I don't have time.

CHUN-NI: A few stitches will do. (*She picks up a sewing kit from the bed.*) Is this the sewing kit I gave you? You've kept it all this time.

(*CHEN HSI nods. CHUN-NI looks at him with satisfaction and sews the tear in his sleeve.*)

CHEN: Chun-ni.

CHUN-NI: Well?

CHEN: Have you returned home since you left?

CHUN-NI: No.

CHEN: Don't you want to see your mother?

CHUN-NI: Of course.

CHEN: When do you plan to go back?

CHUN-NI: Whenever you wish. I'll do as you say.

CHEN: You know the situation here is very tense. I'm afraid I won't have any time to take you around the city.

CHUN-NI: I thought of that, too. When I saw you were so busy I thought of leaving right away, but I felt I had a lot to say to you.

CHEN: What about?

CHUN-NI: But just now I feel at a loss to know what to say. (*Smiles.*)

CHEN: I think you should leave tomorrow, Chun-ni.

CHUN-NI: Are you serious?

CHEN: Yes. Since our unit has just come to the city, I'm afraid the others may have some objections if you stay. When we've settled down, I'll come back home to see you.

CHUN-NI: Chen Hsi, you ... you. ...

CHEN: You'll go back, eh?

(*Music in the Park sounds pressing.*)

CHEN: I must go. (*Stands up.*)

CHUN-NI: Wait a minute. (*Stands up too.*)

CHEN: I don't have time! (*Breaks the thread.*)

CHUN-NI (*holding in her hand the needle and broken thread and looking dismayed*): You . . . Chen Hsi!

CHEN (*stops and looks back*): What's the matter with you, Chun-ni? I've told you the truth. I can't take you with me to every place I go, especially in public. If you're not going back home, stay in the room, and don't go about in the streets.

(*Dumbfounded, CHUN-NI stares at him.*)

CHEN: Now don't be angry; I'll be right back. (*Waving good-bye to her*) See you after a while. (*Exit.*)

CHUN-NI: Chen Hsi! . . . (*Buries her face in her hands and flings herself down on CHEN HSI's bed.*)

(*LU HUA enters carrying an army blanket. He looks puzzled when he sees CHUN-NI's state. He picks up the eggs and handkerchief and goes over to her.*)

LU HUA: What's happened, Chun-ni?

CHUN-NI (*raising her head*): Oh, nothing!

LU HUA: Been quarrelling, eh? Has he treated you badly?

(*A short pause. HUNG MAN-TANG comes into the courtyard.*)

CHUN-NI: I shouldn't have come here disturbing him.

LU HUA (*explaining*): Chen Hsi is pig-headed. He has a rough tongue. If he has done anything wrong you must forgive him, for after all he has a kind heart.

CHUN-NI (*giving the sewing kit to LU HUA*): Look here, he broke this thread. . . .

LU HUA (*astounded*): Really? Where is he?

CHUN-NI: He went to the Park.

LU HUA (*stands up*): I'm going to look for him.

CHUN-NI: Please don't, Instructor — don't interrupt his work.

43

LU HUA (*looking back*): I never thought he could be so unreasonable. Chun-ni, compose yourself and don't be upset.

CHUN-NI: I'm not upset, but I'm worried about him.... You're a good friend of his, Instructor. You always praised him in your letters to me. You told me that he was intelligent, capable, courageous in battle, clever in doing things and that he was a good Communist. I believe you're right but I hope he'll be worthy of the Party's kindness to him.

LU HUA: You're a good Communist too, Chun-ni. To be frank, we know that deep inside he is vain. But I never thought it would show so openly and quickly....

CHUN-NI: All right, Instructor. (*Handing him the sewing kit*) I'll turn this over to you.

LU HUA (*taking the sewing kit*): What? Are you leaving? No, you mustn't. I'd rather take a flogging than let you go. You must not leave now, Chun-ni.

(*Restraining her tears and biting her lips, CHUN-NI drops her head and walks towards the door. HUNG MAN-TANG comes with a pipe in his hand. Seeing him, CHUN-NI turns back, leans against the wall and weeps. HUNG MAN-TANG sucks noisily at his pipe.*)

(*LU TA-CHENG enters.*)

LU TA-CHENG: Lu Hua, I've just made a call on all the squads. Everything's fine in the First and Second Platoons. Here, take a look at the First Platoon's resolutions and the Second Platoon's guarantee. But Chao Ta-ta has sent in a request to Company Headquarters from the Third Platoon, asking to be sent away from the Nanking Road to a place where he can do some fighting. Tung Ah-nan went to have a meal in a cafe with a girl student and hasn't returned yet. What sort of soldiers are they?

HUNG: And there's something worse!

LU TA-CHENG (*puzzled*): What?

HUNG: Chen Hsi thinks Chun-ni is not good enough for him!

LU TA-CHENG: Really?

HUNG (*picking up the cloth socks*): Look, he threw these away!

LU TA-CHENG: So! (*Takes the socks.*) This "fragrant" breeze has got into his marrow. Where is he? (*Prepares to leave.*)

LU HUA: Don't go, Company Commander. Since the three of us are already here, let's have a Party Branch Committee meeting.

LU TA-CHENG: All right. But I think we should also fetch Chen Hsi back and call a membership meeting to give him a good telling-off. (*Puts the socks in his canvas bag.*) Messenger! Messenger!

LU HUA: I'm afraid giving him a telling-off won't solve the problem.

LU TA-CHENG: With so much work on hand, the Third Platoon will certainly fall right here on the Nanking Road if he keeps on acting like this! (*To LU HUA*) Everything would be all right now if we had given the platoon a good talking to long ago. See how you've spoiled them!

HUNG: Company Commander!

CHUN-NI: Comrades, I'm the one who has caused you all this trouble. (*Starts to go.*)

LU HUA: Chun-ni!

CHUN-NI (*looking back*): It's all clear to me now. The work here is just as important as fighting a battle at

45

the front. When I go back I shall do my work happily and support you at the front just the same as I've always done. (*Runs out.*)

LU TA-CHENG
LU HUA } : Chun-ni!

(*Silence.*)

HUNG: Are we going to let her go like this? The peasants fed us with their grain, and carried our things in their wagons to help us cross the Yangtse and come to Shanghai. Are we going to let her go back with tear-filled eyes? What will her fellow-villagers think when they find out what's happened? ... Why hang your heads in silence? If you can't do anything about it, let's write to our superiors and ask them to withdraw us....

LU TA-CHENG: What? Withdraw? That's ridiculous! (*Excitedly*) When I was a squad leader you were already a veteran soldier. You know our company inside out. We've been through all sorts of campaigns, haven't we? We've used all sorts of guns, fought in all sorts of positions. Now withdraw? It's true when I was first told to stand guard on this road, it didn't appeal to me. But now that we're here, we must stick it out. With the leadership of the Party and our superiors, it's impossible for me to believe we can't overcome this "fragrant" breeze of the bourgeoisie on the Nanking Road.

HUNG: Right! Now I feel better!

(*AH-NAN vaults over the wall into the courtyard. When he hears someone talking in the room, he stops and listens.*)

LU TA-CHENG: In my opinion the first thing that should be done in overcoming this "fragrant" breeze is to send Tung Ah-nan back home; otherwise the entire company will be infected. There's no telling whether Chen Hsi has been influenced by that Shanghai soldier or not.

LU HUA: Most of the soldiers from Shanghai are good. They are new blood for our unit though a few of them have weak points.

HUNG: No matter what you say, he's still a new soldier, a kid who comes from a poor family.

LU TA-CHENG: He comes from a poor family, true, but he smells of the old Nanking Road. Otherwise, why does he mix with those bourgeois girl students? (*Makes a motion of driving someone away by tugging at LU HUA's arm.*) Let's send him back before he has a chance to influence the others!

HUNG: I'm against sending Ah-nan away. I think we should first fetch Chen Hsi back and give him a good telling off?

LU HUA: I disagree. We shouldn't send Ah-nan back home or take Chen Hsi to task. Tung Ah-nan comes from the masses. If we don't reform him, the bourgeoisie will try to win him over. To be unable to unite with and educate Tung Ah-nan only proves the ideological weakness in our work here on the Nanking Road. We can't fight an ideological battle in such an over-simplified way. It isn't too late to deal with this problem right now. Why can't we act according to Chairman Mao's directions, carry out class education and "train these soldiers under the enemy's nose"? I think we should act right now. Old Hung, you go and talk to Chun-ni; Company Commander, you go and look for Chen Hsi and I'll fetch Tung Ah-nan. Agreed?

LU TA-CHENG }
HUNG MAN-TANG }: Very good!

MESSENGER (*entering*): Reporting! I couldn't find Tung Ah-nan. (*Going up to LU TA-CHENG*) Company Commander! Chao Ta-ta went off with a girl with long pigtails.

LU TA-CHENG: Nonsense! How could he do such a thing!

MESSENGER: It's true. If you don't believe me, go and see for yourself.

LU TA-CHENG: What a mess! Take me there! (*Upon entering the courtyard, he spies a dark shadow.*) Who's there?

AH-NAN: Tung Ah-nan reporting.

LU TA-CHENG: It's good of you to come back. (*Restraining himself*) All right, go to the barracks. The Old Mess Officer has kept some food for you in the kitchen.

AH-NAN (*explaining*): One of my girl classmates was having trouble and needed my help. She asked me to go out for supper with her and to accompany her to the celebration in the Park. I couldn't refuse her!

LU TA-CHENG: So you couldn't refuse, eh? (*Knowing it's wrong to lose his temper, he speaks gently.*) You're wearing a military uniform — the military uniform of the Chinese People's Liberation Army. D'you understand? A soldier in the Liberation Army must keep in mind the Three Main Rules of Discipline and the Eight Points for Attention;[1] otherwise we'll never win the battle. . . .

---

[1] The Three Main Rules of Discipline are: (1) Obey orders in all your actions. (2) Don't take a single needle or piece of thread from the masses. (3) Turn in everything captured. The Eight Points for Attention are: (1) Speak politely. (2) Pay fairly for what you buy. (3) Return everything you borrow. (4) Pay for anything you damage. (5) Don't hit or swear at people. (6) Don't damage crops. (7) Don't take liberties with women. (8) Don't ill-treat captives.

AH-NAN: There's no need for so much fuss, Company Commander. I only had a meal at the International Hotel!

LU TA-CHENG: Oh, what big talk! You *only* had a meal at the International Hotel! Is the International Hotel the kind of place where we should go?

AH-NAN: Why can't we go there? We're liberated; everybody's equal. If the rich can go there why can't I?

LU TA-CHENG (*caught for an answer at the moment*): Ah, you are a wonderful man! You've defended yourself eloquently! But let me ask you, did you join the army to help the revolution or to enjoy yourself more than others?

AH-NAN: Of course, I want to help the revolution. (*Muttering*) But don't I have the right to go to the International Hotel?

LU TA-CHENG: All right! Go to the International Hotel, and to the coffee bars, dance-halls and other such places. But remember, if you do, you'll not be fit to wear that uniform of yours! (*To the MESSENGER*) Let's go. (*Bustles out with the MESSENGER.*)

AH-NAN (*dumbfounded*): Don't want me any more, eh? I suppose I'm discharged.

(*He enters the barracks, takes off his uniform and folds it up. LU HUA walks towards him.*)

AH-NAN: I'm leaving, Instructor.

LU HUA: Where are you going?

AH-NAN: Now that the country is liberated, I can go any place and still help the revolution. (*Emotionally*) Call me when you need me and I'll come. Good-bye!

LU HUA: Stay where you are!

49

AH-NAN: Oh, yes. (*Holds out the uniform he is carrying in his hand and gives it to the Instructor.*) I shall not forget your friendship. (*He leaves quietly.*)

LU HUA (*astounded*): Come back here, Ah-nan! Put this uniform away, Old Hung. (*Dashes out the door.*) Tung Ah-nan! (*Exit.*)

HUNG: Oh my! He's really left.

(*The stage darkens for a change of scene.*)

SCENE FOUR

In MRS. LIN's living room.

The room is furnished with a sofa, a piano, two chairs, and a combination radio. A picture of LIN YUAN-YUAN and a vase of flowers are on the piano. LO KE-WEN is playing the piano in an angry, moody way. MRS. LIN returns.

MRS. LIN: Ke-wen! Lo Ke-wen!

(LO KE-WEN turns round.)

MRS. LIN: My, you're taking it easy; playing the piano all alone! Where's Yuan-yuan?

(LO KE-WEN shakes his head.)

MRS. LIN: Didn't I tell you to wait for her at the entrance to the Park? Oh, you're good-for-nothing! What shall I do without my Yuan-yuan! I just can't live without her! I even had the cheek to go to the Liberation Army's Art Troupe looking for her.

(LO KE-WEN raises his head.)

MRS. LIN *(shaking her head)*: But they didn't know where she was. And things are very tense outside, just as if there's going to be a battle.

LO: Really? Let it come then! The fiercer the better. Let it come and destroy this world!

MRS. LIN: Ke-wen! Have you taken leave of your senses?

51

LO: This world has no place for me. It makes me feel empty and sad! It has taken away all I love! (*Drops his head and starts to play the piano again.*)

MRS. LIN: Stop playing the piano, will you? You're driving me mad! I'm going to phone the police.

(*CHU MAN-LI enters.*)

MRS. LIN: Ah, it's Man-li!

CHU: Hello, Aunt Lin?

MRS. LIN: You seldom come here these days. How did you find time to come?

CHU: Well, I was passing your house and I saw the lights on, so I thought I'd drop in. (*To LO KE-WEN*) Why are you still up at this hour of the night, Mr. Lo?

LO: I can't sleep. You've come at the right time, Man-li. Come for a stroll with me. I feel as if I'm the only person in the world — I'm so lonely!

CHU: It's raining.

LO: I like to walk in the rain. Let it soak me through and through and then I'll feel better.

CHU: Don't tell me about all your petty-bourgeois sentiments. You can pack up your romanticism. You'd better straighten up and catch up with the times; otherwise you'll be sent off to reform yourself.

LO: You! At school you were only a.... Now you're putting on the airs of a revolutionary!

CHU: Don't get excited, Mr. Lo. I'm only looking after your interests. You are promising. As an artist you should take good care of yourself. When I see you looking so sad all the time I feel sorry and worried about you. Now don't be angry with me; I'm still your good friend. Let's shake hands. I have come here to say good-bye to you.

LO: Where are you going?

CHU: Recently, the Liberation Army has been recruiting girls from our school. Before long I'll be leaving for the front.

MRS. LIN (astounded): Really? How can your mother let you go?

CHU: Of course, she's against it.

MRS. LIN: Does it mean there's really going to be more fighting?

CHU: That's what everyone's saying. You'd better make your plans now.

MRS. LIN (alarmed): What about Yuan-yuan? Will the Liberation Army take her, too?

CHU: That's hard to say. Just now at the Park she spoke to me about going to Nanking to take the entrance examination for the Military and Political College. Besides she's going there with a boy friend!

MRS. LIN: My goodness! Has she gone already?

CHU: Not yet. I saw her walking down the street just now and her boy friend was still with her!

MRS. LIN: Hurry! Go and look for her, Ke-wen!

LO: All right! When I come back we must leave Shanghai immediately. Will you please show me the way, Man-li.

(LO KE-WEN and CHU MAN-LI go out together.)

MRS. LIN: Wait a minute! Fat Ma, bring me Yuan-yuan's raincoat, rubber shoes and woollen sweater.

FAT MA (entering): You don't have to worry, Madame, your daughter will certainly come back.

MRS. LIN: Of course, you're not worried — she's not your daughter.

FAT MA: It's a different world now. Nothing will happen to your daughter with the Liberation Army around.

She'll never be kidnapped and made a child bride as I was when I was a girl.

MRS. LIN: Fat Ma, you'd better keep away from politics. My way of life has always been to eat and sleep and not to ask any questions about world affairs. (*Starts to leave.*)

FAT MA: Madame, there's a letter for you. (*Hands her the letter.*)

MRS. LIN (*opens the letter and looks shocked*): Fat Ma! (*Holds the letter as if it were a bomb.*)

FAT MA: What's the matter, Madame?

MRS. LIN: Where did this letter come from?

FAT MA: A man wearing a felt hat brought it.

MRS. LIN: During the next few days you must be careful. You must see that all doors and windows are closed and locked. I hear the Liberation Army is going to withdraw.

FAT MA: I think that's just a rumour.

MRS. LIN: What do you know about it? Drat you! (*The front door bell rings.*)

MRS. LIN: Hurry and see who's at the door, Fat Ma.

FAT MA: Who's there?

(*Off-stage: "It's me! Open the door quick, Fat Ma!"*)

FAT MA: Your daughter's come back, Madame.

MRS. LIN: Hurry up and open the door, hurry! (*Exit FAT MA.*)

MRS. LIN (*mutters to herself*): Thank Heaven! (*After a short while, LIN YUAN-YUAN strolls in.*)

YUAN-YUAN: Mama, I'm back.

(*MRS. LIN ignores her.*)

YUAN-YUAN: But I'm leaving again.

MRS. LIN (*turning round hurriedly*): Yuan-yuan, my darling, don't break my heart again! (*Grabbing hold of*

YUAN-YUAN) You're the only one I have in the world. I left your father for your sake. Now, you mustn't desert me!

YUAN-YUAN: What's wrong with me, Mama? I swear I've done nothing wrong.

MRS. LIN: Hush your nonsense. See how wet you are. Hurry up and change into some dry clothes. Put on your sweater.

YUAN-YUAN: Wait a minute, Mama! Look who's here! (*Goes out of the door.*) Come in. (*Pulls AH-NAN into the room.*)

(*AH-NAN looks somewhat out of place. MRS. LIN is taken aback.*)

MRS. LIN: It's you?

(*AH-NAN turns to go. LIN YUAN-YUAN stands in his path.*)

YUAN-YUAN: Is he welcome, Mama? He saw me home. I want him to stay here tonight. Do you agree? I know you'll agree. Am I right? (*A short pause. MRS. LIN doesn't express her attitude.*) If you don't, then I'll see him home. Let's go, Ah-nan.

MRS. LIN: Yuan-yuan!

YUAN-YUAN: Do you agree? If you do, then prepare a place for him to sleep.

(*MRS. LIN stands up unwillingly.*)

YUAN-YUAN: Please go and prepare a place, Mama dear. (*LIN YUAN-YUAN pushes MRS. LIN out of the room.*)

AH-NAN: It seems as if I'm dreaming.... (*Attempts to go.*)

YUAN-YUAN: What's the matter, Ah-nan? Why don't you sit down?

AH-NAN: Is this your home, Yuan-yuan?

YUAN-YUAN: Yes.

AH-NAN: I'm leaving.

YUAN-YUAN: Is it right for you to bring me back home, then leave me here alone? (*Pushes him down on a chair.*) Look, here are some sweets. Do you like music?

(*AH-NAN nods.*)

YUAN-YUAN (*switching on the radio*): This is called "Nocturne". If you keep quiet and listen, it'll carry you away into the silver clouds! Ah-nan, you must know that right now I'm at the crossroads of my life. I want to leave this house for ever. I'm also tired of the celebration in the Park and beating drums. Can you help me?

(*AH-NAN, not knowing what to say, smiles.*)

YUAN-YUAN: It would be really good if I were like you — in the Liberation Army with a rifle across my shoulder patrolling the Nanking Road, especially late at night when everyone's sleeping and the Huangpu River is flowing quietly. The only noise is made by the shuffling boots of the Liberation Army soldiers. What are you thinking about, Ah-nan? Are you tired or ill? I'll let you have a rest, all right?

AH-NAN: I'd like to tell you something, Yuan-yuan! I hope you'll help me. I've left the Liberation Army.

YUAN-YUAN: Really? Why?

AH-NAN: I don't know.

YUAN-YUAN: Can't you do anything about going back?

(*AH-NAN shakes his head.*)

(*Silence.*)

YUAN-YUAN: What do you plan to do?

AH-NAN: Go to work in a factory.

YUAN-YUAN (*suddenly breaks into a smile*): No, let's go to Nanking.

AH-NAN: What'll we do there?

YUAN-YUAN: Take the entrance examination to the Military and Political College.

AH-NAN: Take the entrance examination to the Military and Political College? (*Feeling a glimmer of hope*) Am I eligible?

YUAN-YUAN: Of course you are. Let's go, Ah-nan. There's no better time than now. It's much more romantic to go to the Military and Political College than to stand guard here on the Nanking Road. Just think, in the College we can read, sing, ride horses, fight ... and we can help and encourage each other, too. ...

AH-NAN (*shaking her hand*): Do you really mean it, Yuan-yuan?

YUAN-YUAN: Honestly I do.

AH-NAN: Thank you for showing me a way out, Yuan-yuan!

YUAN-YUAN: Will you go?

AH-NAN: Yes, I will.

YUAN-YUAN: All right then, I'll come to tell you when it's time to leave. (*Shakes his hand.*)

MRS. LIN (*entering*): It's time to go to bed! Fat Ma, show the guest to his room.

(*Exit FAT MA with AH-NAN.*)

MRS. LIN: What's the relation between you and Ah-nan, Yuan-yuan?

YUAN-YUAN (*pondering*): We're just friends.

MRS. LIN: Will you please listen to me, Yuan-yuan? Don't see him again; if you do I shall die before your very eyes!

YUAN-YUAN: What's the matter with you, Mama?

57

MRS. LIN: You know the Liberation Army won't be in Shanghai long. I heard they are going to take girl students to the front.

YUAN-YUAN: Who said that, Mama?

MRS. LIN: You don't need to know that. Promise me you won't see that Liberation Army soldier again.

YUAN-YUAN: All right, if you promise to give me some money to help him go inland.

MRS. LIN: Why?

YUAN-YUAN: He's quit the Liberation Army and wants to go to the interior.

MRS. LIN (*surprised*): What?! He's quit the Liberation Army and you've hidden him in my house and are going to give him money too! Yuan-yuan, you're bringing trouble upon yourself! Go and tell him to leave here immediately!

YUAN-YUAN: Listen to me, Mama. . . .

MRS. LIN: If you don't I'll go myself.

YUAN-YUAN: Mama!

MRS. LIN: Get out of the way!
(*LO KE-WEN enters hurriedly.*)

LO: Yuan-yuan. . . .

MRS. LIN: You've come at the right time, Ke-wen. (*To YUAN-YUAN*) Tell your cousin what you plan to do!

LO: . . . What's up, Aunt?

MRS. LIN: I think it's best to let her friend speak for himself.

YUAN-YUAN (*blocking her path*): Mama!
(*Hardly has MRS. LIN pushed LIN YUAN-YUAN aside than AH-NAN enters.*)
(*Silence.*)

AH-NAN: I've heard everything you said.

58

LO: What are you, a soldier, doing here? Why do you come here in the middle of the night and disturb the peace of the family?

(*AH-NAN attempts to go, but LIN YUAN-YUAN blocks his way.*)

YUAN-YUAN: Where are your manners, Cousin? I invited him to come here!

LO: What did you bring him here for, Yuan-yuan? Don't you know we've never had anything to do with soldiers.

MRS. LIN: Besides he's a deserter! What if they come here looking for him?

YUAN-YUAN (*with tears in her eyes*): Stop insulting him!

(*AH-NAN starts to explain but thinks better of it and runs out.*)

YUAN-YUAN: Ah-nan!

LO: Yuan-yuan! (*Blocks her way.*)

(*LIN YUAN-YUAN weeps.*)

LO: Yuan-yuan! (*Stepping closer to her*) I really was worried about you! Do you want to give up everything and destroy yourself? I'm not against your being revolutionary and progressive. If you have ability and a good voice the revolution will use you. But it's really difficult to understand why you mix with such people. (*Tenderly*) Yuan-yuan, you should take good care of yourself. Calm down and listen to what I have to say. You must come back home, go to school and work hard to train your voice. I've been feeling sad and empty these last two months. I seem to have lost my heart. I don't know what to do. The piano is my only companion. But now the peace in this little paradise of mine has been broken too! I always seem to hear someone knocking on my door at night warning me that if I'm not careful I'll be sent off to reform myself.

MRS. LIN: Is that so?

LO: I think Ah-nan's presence here may have something to do with it.

MRS. LIN: Good heavens! No wonder I received this letter. Read it. (*Gives LO KE-WEN the anonymous letter.*) Someone's warning us.

LO (*after reading the letter*): Ah-nan was definitely sent here by the local police to investigate.

MRS. LIN: Let's hurry and leave here, my darling daughter!

LO: The sooner we leave Shanghai the better, Aunt. Let's go, Yuan-yuan!

YUAN-YUAN: Damn! Damn! I hate everything in this house. From now on you go your way and I'll go mine. (*Runs out.*)

LO: Yuan-yuan! (*Flings himself down upon the sofa.*)

MRS. LIN: Yuan-yuan! (*Chases after her.*)

(*The stage darkens for a change of scene.*)

SCENE FIVE

Light music attracts people to a secluded spot in the Park.

Red and green lights are strung from tree to tree. The celebration in the Park is about to end.

Ill at ease, AH-HSIANG is pacing up and down in front of a bench. A short while later, CHAO TA-TA enters.

CHAO: All right. There's no one here but you and I.

AH-HSIANG: I... I feel that someone's after me. I'm a bit afraid.

CHAO: If the sky falls down I'll hold it up. Now, out with it!

AH-HSIANG: You're not to breathe a word about this to anyone. It doesn't matter if I die; but my conscience won't allow me to let the Liberation Army men be involved in this.

CHAO: You have my word on that.

AH-HSIANG (*looking around*): Tonight at twelve o'clock the boss is going to take me to Hongkong to sell me to a rich man.

CHAO: Why?

AH-HSIANG: To pay a debt owed by my family. The boss said that if I could get my younger brother to go to the Soochow River to see him the debt would be cancelled. And he also agreed to give me some money.

CHAO: The boss? Who's the boss?

AH-HSIANG: The ring-leader; he's a gangster. I heard that he is in contact with the Americans.

CHAO (*gripping AH-HSIANG by the arm*): Where is he? Lead me there.

AH-HSIANG: Let me go. I risked my life coming here to tell you this. So please keep quiet about it, or all my family will suffer. I must ask a favour of you: tell Ah-nan not to come home tonight. (*Turns to go.*)

CHAO: This won't do! I can't just stand by and watch them drag you off to Hongkong and do nothing to stop them. What sort of person is this ring-leader? Is he the one who beat you on the Nanking Road that time? (*Stamping his foot*) I want an answer!

AH-HSIANG: I'm afraid.... (*Dodging away from him.*)

CHAO (*bellowing*): Come back!

AH-HSIANG: Let me go!

CHAO: Don't be afraid, just because I have a loud voice.

AH-HSIANG: No — you're a good man.

CHAO: Let's go! (*Seizes her by the arm.*) You point him out to me. I won't let anyone know that you've told me.

AH-HSIANG: Someone's coming. (*Wrenches free and runs.*)

(*CHAO TA-TA turns round and comes face to face with the MESSENGER and LU TA-CHENG.*)

LU TA-CHENG: Oho, Chao Ta-ta! You certainly know how to pick a good place — plenty of grass and flowers!

CHAO: Company Commander!

LU TA-CHENG: No need for any explanations — I saw it all. Well, what are you going to do?

CHAO: I'm going to the Nanking Road to look for someone. (*Turns to go.*)

LU TA-CHENG: Really? Is someone waiting there for you?

CHAO (*nodding*): Yes. I have something important to attend to.

LU TA-CHENG: Hey, Chao Ta-ta. I never expected you to get caught by a pair of Nanking Road pigtails. No wonder you've been going around with a dreamy look on your face the last few days. I thought you really couldn't get used to the Nanking Road and wanted to go to the front. But it seems that I'm in the dark. You're one of our old comrades. You should think of me. You know how I feel.... As a Communist we should put all our effort into guarding this road! But you....

CHAO: Company Commander, I know that since coming here to Shanghai there's been a lot wrong with my thinking. I know now that my original ideas were wrong. I acknowledge my faults and hope my superiors will criticize me.

LU TA-CHENG: Since you're able to change your mind, you're still a good comrade. Let's go!

CHAO: But you must let me see her tonight.

LU TA-CHENG: What? You still haven't changed your mind after all I've said! (*Commanding*) Chao Ta-ta!

63

CHAO: Present!

LU TA-CHENG: I sanction your request.

CHAO: Please return my application, Company Commander. I'm not going anywhere else.

LU TA-CHENG: Go back right now and pack your things. You're leaving the Nanking Road immediately for the front!

CHAO: But something's afoot here!

LU TA-CHENG (*stunned by CHAO TA-TA's serious attitude*): What's afoot?

CHAO: That girl who was here just now is Ah-nan's elder sister. She said someone is forcing her to go to Hongkong tonight. Are we going to stand by and do nothing to save her?

LU TA-CHENG: Is that true?

CHAO (*almost in tears*): Have I ever lied to you, Company Commander?

LU TA-CHENG: Ah! Why didn't you say so before. Hurry, fetch her back here!

CHAO: Yes. (*Exit.*)

LU TA-CHENG: So I'm the one who's short of brains. (*To the MESSENGER*) What did you see when you made the report?

MESSENGER: I . . . I wasn't clear myself.
(*CHAO TA-TA enters.*)

CHAO: She ran away in fear. Let's go to her house.

LU TA-CHENG: Let's go and report this to our superiors. Let's go! (*All three go out.*)
(*It starts drizzling. AH-NAN enters hurriedly. When he hears someone behind him shouting "Ah-nan!" he turns and disappears into the trees.*)
(*LU HUA dashes on.*)

LU HUA: Tung Ah-nan! Ah-nan!

. (*AH-JUNG entering at a trot.*)

AH-JUNG: Comrade of the Liberation Army! Have you seen Ah-nan?

LU HUA: I'm looking for him.

AH-JUNG: I ran into his sister just now; she told me to tell Ah-nan not to go home tonight.

LU HUA: Why?

AH-JUNG: She asked me to tell him to be a good soldier and avenge Ah-hsiang!

LU HUA (*bewildered*): Avenge her? What has happened?

AH-JUNG: I don't know.

LU HUA: Show me her house.

AH-JUNG: All right.

(*LU HUA goes out with AH-JUNG. AH-NAN appears.*)

AH-NAN: My sister wants me to avenge her? What! (*Starts to go.*)

(*LIN YUAN-YUAN runs on stage.*)

YUAN-YUAN: Don't be angry with me, Ah-nan. I apologize for everything. I had a big row with my family after you left. Let's leave right away, Ah-nan!

AH-NAN: I must go . home first.

YUAN-YUAN: Don't hesitate again, Ah-nan!

CHU MAN-LI (*suddenly emerging from the shadows*): Let him go, Yuan-yuan. Don't worry, there'll still be time after the celebration in the Park is over. I'll buy tickets for you and see you to the train as well.

YUAN-YUAN: Good! Then I'll meet you the day after tomorrow in the same old place. So long.

AH-NAN: Good-bye. (*Runs out.*)

CHU: Yuan-yuan, I'm really moved by your behaviour. You're just like a petrel in a storm. (*Locks arms with her and they go out together.*)
(*The rain begins to pour.   Lights glimmer in the distance.*)

(*The stage darkens for a change of scene.*)

SCENE SIX

*On the bank of the Soochow River at TUNG AH-
NAN's home.*

*Midnight. The clock of the Custom House strikes
twelve.*

*In the distance are shacks, street lights and the
shadow of a tall building.*

*A meat-dumpling vendor passes under the street
light.*

MAMA TUNG enters hurriedly.

VENDOR: Why are you just coming home at this
hour?

MAMA TUNG: I went to see Uncle Chou about something, but he wasn't in.

VENDOR: Was it about Ah-hsiang's affair?

(*MAMA TUNG nods.*)

(*The MEAT-DUMPLING VENDOR passes on.
MAMA TUNG goes into the hut and lights the lamp.*)

(*THUG A shadows and keeps a watch on MAMA
TUNG, followed by THUG B.*)

THUG B: Here comes a soldier!

THUG A: Is it Ah-nan?

THUG B: Looks like him. Let's act now!

THUG A: Wait a minute! It's too risky. We better
let Ah-hsiang bring him out to the sampan first!

(*Exeunt.*)

(*AH-JUNG enters with Political Instructor LU HUA. The MESSENGER follows them.*)

AH-JUNG: Here we are, Instructor. This is Ah-nan's home.

(*MAMA TUNG comes out of the house carrying a small bundle.*)

AH-JUNG: Someone's come to see you, Mama Tung. Instructor, this is Mama Tung. Mama Tung, this is the political instructor on the Nanking Road and Ah-nan's superior.

MAMA TUNG: Good evening, Officer!

LU HUA: How do you do, Mama Tung?

(*The two go into the house. The MESSENGER stands on guard outside the door.*)

AH-JUNG: I'm going to get my newspapers, Instructor. I'll come back here for you as soon as I have distributed them. See you later. (*Exit.*)

MAMA TUNG: Sit down, Officer.

LU HUA: Mama Tung, my name's Lu. You may call me Comrade Lu.

MAMA TUNG: Oh, sit down, Comrade Lu. What has brought you here so late?

LU HUA: Has Ah-nan been home today?

MAMA TUNG: No.

LU HUA: Didn't Ah-hsiang go to look for him?

MAMA TUNG: Yes, she did.

LU HUA: Why did she want to find him?

MAMA TUNG: Please don't laugh at us when I tell you the truth, Comrade Lu. We're so poor. We were hoping Ah-nan would come back tonight to help us out of some trouble.

LU HUA: What's the matter, Mama Tung? You can tell me; I'm a good friend of Ah-nan.

68

MAMA TUNG (*hesitatingly*): We owe money borrowed at a terrible rate of interest and we can't possibly pay it.

LU HUA: A loan? How much is it?

MAMA TUNG (*covering up*): Not much. (*Turns round and picks up her small bundle.*) You stay here, Comrade Lu, I'll be right back.

LU HUA: What are you trying to do, Mama Tung?

MAMA TUNG: We really have no way out. This is his father's fur-lined jacket. I'm going to....

LU HUA (*taking the bundle from her*): I have some money here. (*Holding it out to her*) See if it's enough to settle your debt.

MAMA TUNG: No, no! I can't take your money. The Government has given us money twice already.

LU HUA: Take it, Mama Tung. This is not my money.... It's Ah-nan's.

MAMA TUNG: Ah-nan's?

LU HUA: This is the savings from Ah-nan's monthly allowance that I have been keeping for him. (*Thrusts the money into her hand.*)

MAMA TUNG: Really?

LU HUA: Yes. Ah-nan asked me to bring it to you.

MAMA TUNG (*tears swelling in her eyes*): I never thought that he.... Comrade, this money is a life-saver! (*Kneels down.*)

LU HUA (*hurriedly helping her up*): Don't feel sad, Mama Tung.

MAMA TUNG: I... I'm happy. I never dreamed that I would meet such a good comrade as you. Oh, please wait, I'm going to buy a bowl of meat dumplings for you.

LU HUA: I'm not hungry, Mama Tung. What's happened to Ah-hsiang?

MAMA TUNG: Someone is forcing her to go to Hongkong because of this debt.

LU HUA: Who is he?

MAMA TUNG: Old Seven, the owner of a dance-hall.

LU HUA: Where is he?

MAMA TUNG: In a sampan on the Soochow River, waiting for Ah-nan to return. He said that if he can meet Ah-nan, the debt and all the other things will be settled. I fear something will happen to Ah-nan. There's no need for him to come back now. Things have turned out all right for Ah-hsiang. . . . You wait, I'll be right back. (*Exit.*)

LU HUA (*extremely puzzled*): Why should Old Seven try to force Ah-hsiang to go to Hongkong? Who is he? Why is he willing to settle everything if he can see Ah-nan? This is most unusual. What are the things to be settled? Why does Old Seven want Ah-nan to go to a sampan on the Soochow River? This is a strange case! Messenger!

MESSENGER: Present! (*Enters the room.*)

LU HUA: Ring up the Company Commander and tell him something has happened here!

MESSENGER: Yes, Instructor! (*Exit.*)

(*AH-HSIANG pushes open the door and enters.*)

AH-HSIANG (*shouting*): Brother! Please hurry up and go!

(*LU HUA turns round. AH-HSIANG stands there dumb-founded.*)

LU HUA: You're Ah-hsiang, aren't you? (*AH-HSIANG nods.*) Your mother told me someone is forcing you to go to Hongkong.

70

AH-HSIANG: That's true, Comrade! What have you come here for?

LU HUA: I'm Ah-nan's good friend and comrade. Ah-nan has just quit his post. Please tell me everything you know about his quitting.

AH-HSIANG: Hurry up and go! Tell Ah-nan not to come home tonight! Someone's going to kill him!

LU HUA: Who? Old Seven?

AH-HSIANG: I hear there's another man called Old K!

LU HUA. Old K? Where is he?

AH-HSIANG: On the Soochow River.

LU HUA: Take me there.

AH-HSIANG: Oh no! There's a gang there. Originally they tried to trick me into taking my brother there so they could murder him! (*Crying*) I almost fell for their trick. . . . Comrade, tell my brother to be a good soldier. As long as he's in the Liberation Army, I'll have a chance to live. Hurry and go now! (*Turns round.*)

LU HUA: Where are you going, Ah-hsiang?

AH-HSIANG: I'm going to Hongkong with them.

LU HUA: Come back here! You must not jump into the fire!

AH-HSIANG: Let me go. It doesn't matter if I die, I don't want my brother and you comrades to be involved in this. Hurry and leave here!
(*Under the street lamp, OLD SEVEN is seen directing THUGS A, B, and C. They charge into the house, put out the light and struggle with LU HUA.*)

AH-HSIANG (*dashing out*): Comrades of the Liberation Army!

71

(*OLD SEVEN puts his hand over her mouth to stop her.*)

THUG B (*pointing to LU HUA who is lying on the floor*): He's out!

THUG A: Ah! We've been tricked. This is not Ah-nan — it's an officer!

OLD SEVEN: Damn it! Put him in this burlap bag! (*The voice of a hawker selling boiled eggs is heard.*)

OLD SEVEN: We don't have time; someone's coming along. (*To AH-HSIANG*) So you went to contact the Liberation Army. Throw her in the Soochow River! (*The thugs carry AH-HSIANG away.*) (*LU HUA regains consciousness and gives chase. MAMA TUNG enters carrying a bowl of meat dumplings.*)

MAMA TUNG: Comrade Lu! (*Lights the lamp.*) Where are you? (*Shouting*) Comrade Lu! Ah! That's too bad, he's gone away without eating his meat dumplings. (*Turns round and sees AH-NAN standing at the door.*) Ah-nan!

AH-NAN (*rushing forward*): Mama!

MAMA TUNG (*putting down the bowl of meat dumplings and catching hold of AH-NAN*): Ah-nan, my son! Let me have a look at you!

AH-NAN: What's happened?

MAMA TUNG: Everything's all right now. Fortunately, you sent that money. We can save your sister Ah-hsiang. I'll go and pay off that debt the first thing in the morning.

AH-NAN: Money? Who brought it to you?

MAMA TUNG: Why, didn't you give some money to Comrade Lu to bring here for you?

AH-NAN: My money?

MAMA TUNG: Yes, look! (*Takes out the money.*) This money is a life-saver.

AH-NAN: His name was Lu? What sort of a person was he?

MAMA TUNG: Ah-jung said he was the political instructor on the Nanking Road and your superior!

AH-NAN: Ah, Instructor Lu!

MAMA TUNG: Yes. He said this money was what you saved from your allowance.

AH-NAN: Where is he, Mama?

MAMA TUNG: He was here just now. What's the matter with you, Ah-nan?

AH-NAN: I . . . I. . . . (*Paces the room distractedly, then takes a chair and sits down.*)

MAMA TUNG: Have you wronged someone, Ah-nan? Are you in trouble?

AH-NAN: Oh, I'm so sorry! (*Buries his head in his hands.*)

(*AH-JUNG dashes in.*)

AH-JUNG: Mama Tung! (*Sees Ah-nan.*) Ah-nan! Old Seven has thrown Ah-hsiang into the Soochow River!

MAMA TUNG }
AH-NAN   } : Oh, no.

AH-JUNG: Luckily, the instructor and some boatmen jumped into the river and saved her.

AH-NAN: Take me there!

AH-JUNG: All right. (*Just as he turns to go, LU HUA enters carrying AH-HSIANG.*)

MAMA TUNG: Ah-hsiang!

LU HUA (*hurriedly putting AH-HSIANG down on a long chair made of wicker*): Hurry. Take her to the hospital! They'll look after her. (*Suddenly seeing Ah-nan*) It's you, Ah-nan!

73

AH-NAN: I'm ashamed to face you, Instructor. . . . Where're you going?

LU HUA: After Old Seven!

AH-NAN: But you're wounded. Let me go!

LU HUA: You've taken off your uniform, left the company and don't have a weapon; what's the use of your going?

AH-NAN: I'm going to report to the Company Commander!

LU HUA: Someone has already been sent. It's best for you to stay here and think over carefully what you've done. (*Goes out in pursuit of OLD SEVEN.*)

AH-NAN: Take care of Ah-hsiang, Mama. Instructor! (*Runs after him.*)

(*Voice of the MESSENGER off-stage: "Here's the house, Company Commander."*)

(*LU TA-CHENG enters at the head of CHEN HSI, CHAO TA-TA and others. The MESSENGER shows them into the room.*)

MESSENGER: This is Ah-nan's mother.

LU TA-CHENG: We're late, Mama Tung.

CHAO (*going over to AH-HSIANG*): Oh!

LU TA-CHENG (*to CHEN HSI*): Well, Platoon Leader Chen, do you still think all's quiet on the Nanking Road?

CHEN (*hesitatingly*): I never thought. . . . (*Lowers his head.*)

LU TA-CHENG: There're many things you haven't thought of! You stay here, Chao Ta-ta. The rest of you come with me!

CHAO: Why am I to stay here, Company Commander?

LU TA-CHENG: Take Ah-hsiang to the hospital immediately!

CHAO: I . . . I. . . .

LU TA-CHENG: I told you that you're short of brains.
. . . Let's go!

(*The stage darkens for a change of scene.*)

SCENE SEVEN

In the courtyard of the barracks. Hanging from trees in a grove is a banner with the words "Welcome Party" written on it. CHEN HSI and fighters of the Eighth Squad are sitting around with piles of peanuts and sweets before them. Everyone looks serious, waiting for the party to begin.

LU TA-CHENG enters.

LU TA-CHENG: What's wrong? Why are you sitting around with such long faces? You look as if you're waiting to denounce a person, not welcome him. (*Imperatively*) Chen Hsi, tell your men to eat the sweets and peanuts. Did you hear me? This is an order!

CHEN (*pouting and looking around perfunctorily at everyone*): Eat! All of you who want to eat, eat.

LU TA-CHENG: And those of you who don't want to eat, don't eat, eh? You take the lead!

CHEN: I don't feel like eating. (*Upon seeing the company commander glaring at him, he orders CHAO TA-TA.*) You're the squad leader, Chao Ta-ta, you eat first.

CHAO: I don't understand why we are having a welcome party and a social get-together instead of punishing someone for running away.

76

LU TA-CHENG: It doesn't matter whether you understand or not. You don't seem to have paid much attention to what the instructor has said.

CHAO: I can't bring myself to welcome anyone!

LU TA-CHENG: You must. (*Pause.*) You're taking a decision of the Party branch too lightly! Why are you sitting there with your head down, Chen Hsi? When the soldier ran away you were having fun in the Park; when he comes back your head droops! What a platoon leader! Give me your attention, everybody! I'll give a lead. Let's sing the song *March of the Chinese People's Liberation Army.* (*Gives the pitch.*) "Forward, forward, forward. . . ." (*Because the pitch is off key and too high, everybody laughs.*) Let's be serious. You give the pitch, Chao Ta-ta!

CHAO (*immediately begins to sing*): "Forward, forward, forward. . . ."

LU TA-CHENG: Ready? Let's go! "Forward, forward, forward. . . ."

(*Under the direction of the company commander everyone begins to sing loudly.*)

(*LU HUA enters. His head is still in bandages. He looks on the company commander's action with favour.*)

LU HUA: You have really got what it takes, Company Commander.

LU TA-CHENG: Since I was the one who drove Ahnan away, I must take the lead in welcoming him back. Where is he?

LU HUA: He went to the mess hall and won't come out.

LU TA-CHENG: Shall I go and fetch him?

LU HUA: There's no need. I've invited Mama Tung and Uncle Chou. Let's go and welcome them first.

77

LU TA-CHENG: Very good! (*Speaking to all*) Follow me! Let's go to welcome Mama Tung!

(*Headed by the company commander, the fighters march out of the grove singing. HUNG MAN-TANG comes out to meet them.*)

LU HUA: How are you coming along with him?

HUNG: Ah-nan won't budge an inch. No matter what I say he won't come out.

LU HUA: You haven't got what it takes.

HUNG: All right, I'll give him something to eat and let him sleep in my room tonight. He'll be ready to drill and to attend class with the rest of the fighters tomorrow morning. That'll be the end of it.

LU HUA: No, we can't do that. What do you think we invited his mother and Uncle Chou for?

HUNG: To give you a helping hand. Right?

LU HUA: Right! How can we let him miss this political lesson? I now think I know the way of Shanghai soldiers; they won't do anything that hurts their pride. All right, what do you say to letting him welcome his mother with us instead of our welcoming him?

HUNG: You really know something about psychology, Instructor.

LU HUA: Tell him his mother and Uncle Chou have come.

HUNG (*sticking up his thumb*): You're really great, Instructor. (*Goes out smiling.*)

(*The beat of drums and gongs is heard in the courtyard. The MESSENGER enters hurriedly.*)

MESSENGER: Instructor, the guests are here.

LU HUA: Invite them in.

(*After a short time, LU TA-CHENG enters with MAMA TUNG and CHOU TEH-KUEI. LU HUA goes to greet them.*)

MAMA TUNG (*handing him a box of gifts*): Please accept my compliments, Instructor.

LU HUA: We appreciate your kindness very much, Mama Tung, but you'd better keep this for Ah-hsiang.

MAMA TUNG: No, Instructor. I have nothing else with which to express my gratitude to the Liberation Army. . . .

CHOU: It isn't the gift that counts, but the feeling behind it. Please accept it, Instructor.

MAMA TUNG: And here's that money; I don't need it now.

LU HUA: No, no, Mama Tung. . . .

MAMA TUNG: I know now, Instructor — Ah-nan told me everything. If it weren't for you all, I couldn't have saved Ah-hsiang no matter how much money I'd had. How can I accept your money when I haven't yet repaid your kindness in saving my daughter's life?

LU HUA: If you'd treat me like a friend, Mama Tung, please accept the money as a gift from our company for Ah-hsiang's hospital fee.

LU TA-CHENG: This money is the instructor's reward as a disabled armyman. Since he wants to give it to you, please accept it.

MAMA TUNG: Instructor and Comrades, what should I say. (*Wipes away her tears.*)

LU TA-CHENG: Don't feel sad, Mama Tung.

MAMA TUNG: I'm not sad. I'm happy.... (*Tears stream from her eyes. She ponders as she wipes away her tears.*) It would be really nice if Ah-nan's father were alive today.

(HUNG MAN-TANG comes in with AH-NAN.)

LU HUA: Was Ah-nan's father also killed by the reactionaries, Mama Tung?

MAMA TUNG *(nodding)*: Ai! At the time Uncle Chou and Ah-nan's father were working in the same factory. He was killed here on the Nanking Road by the reactionaries in the struggle against foreigners!

CHOU: When you mention the Nanking Road, Comrades, there's no end to what can be said. During my fifty years of life, I've seen the Britishers, Japanese and Yankees rape, burn, kill and run amok here on the Nanking Road. Heaven knows how many revolutionary comrades and workers have lost their lives right here on the Nanking Road! From the Race Course to the Bund, every brick in the streets has been stained with the blood of our martyrs. Some capitalists say the Nanking Road is built on piles of imperialist dollars and pounds. I say, it isn't! This road was built by our own labouring people and has been soaked with the blood of the martyrs! I remember....

(FLASH BACK)

A formation of British troops haughtily marches to the beat of drums. People wearing skull caps and pigtails scuttle out of the way, bow and scatter. A ricksha-driver, who doesn't get out of the way in time, is bayoneted by a British soldier.

The song "Down with the Imperialist Powers" rings out and the air is filled with fluttering red flags. A formation of workers dressed in shabby clothes march arm in arm towards the British soldiers. The British soldiers open fire. The workers fall one after the other. In the end there is only one worker left. That is AH-

NAN's father TUNG AH-TA. He stands up, waves a big red flag and charges towards the British robbers.

It is snowing. Carrying little AH-NAN in her arms and leading AH-HSIANG by the hand, MAMA TUNG slowly walks away.

MAMA TUNG (*off-stage*): During the winter one year when the Japanese troops came, Uncle Chou and Ah-nan's father were sacked by the factory. Ah-nan's father frequently left home for long periods of time. Carrying Ah-nan in my arm and leading Ah-hsiang by the hand, I was forced to go around begging for food on the Nanking Road. Several years later, Ah-nan's father came back home for good and once again we were reunited. Then the American troops came.

CHOU (*off-stage*): Working hand in glove with the imperialists, Chiang Kai-shek, the leader of the counter-revolutionaries, once again occupied Shanghai in the summer of that year. Uniting our fellow countrymen and, in coordination with the victories in the Liberated Areas, we workers held demonstrations and went on strike. Ah-nan's father and I took part in the strikes. Just when Ah-nan's father was leading the workers against the American soldiers, the head of the Kuomintang secret police came on the scene. He's that man called Old K who has now gone underground here on the Nanking Road!

(*American marching music off-stage.*)

(*TUNG AH-TA parts with MAMA TUNG and runs off.*)

(*A group of noisy American soldiers scramble out of a jeep. Several boy and girl students surround the American soldiers. They shout "Go home, Yankees!"*

*The American soldiers try to stop it. A girl student
rushes forward and an American soldier seizes her.
When she struggles to free herself the American soldier
bayonets her.)*

*(TUNG AH-TA leads a crowd of people. OLD K brings
the police. Whistles are heard everywhere. A rifle
cracks and TUNG AH-TA falls to the ground. CHOU
TEH-KUEI comes and helps TUNG AH-TA to his
feet. The crowd scatters. Covered with blood TUNG
AH-TA stands up. CHOU TEH-KUEI hurries to rally
the people for another assault. OLD K flees in terror.
MAMA TUNG runs forward and puts her arms around
TUNG AH-TA. . . .)*

CHOU: That was how Ah-nan's father gave his life here
on the Nanking Road. I shall never forget the way
Mama Tung cried when we went to get his body back.

AH-NAN (*falling down on his knees before MAMA
TUNG and weeping bitterly*): Mama!

MAMA TUNG (*caressing AH-NAN's head*): We're
finally liberated. (*To AH-NAN*) The Liberation Army
has taken you in because of what your father did. I
never dreamed that you'd do such a dreadful thing!
Is taking off your uniform a way to show respect for
your dead father? You're living in happier times, but
you don't appreciate it.

CHOU: You mustn't let your father shed his blood in
vain. Stand firmly on the spot where he shed his blood.
Let it bring new life.

LU HUA: Comrades! Let's always remember the words
of our elders. In standing guard here on this road, we
must carry on the revolutionary cause of our ancestors
who have shed blood and given their lives for us.

82

(*Carrying AH-NAN's uniform, the MESSENGER solemnly walks over to the political instructor.*)

LU HUA (*taking the uniform*): We have kept this uniform for you ever since you took it off. We have also washed it, hoping that you would come back to wear it again. The uniform was won with the blood of innumerable martyrs! Put it on and wear it for the rest of your life!

(*AH-NAN accepts the uniform with tears welling in his eyes.*)

CHAO (*stepping towards AH-NAN to hand him his Sten-gun*): Welcome back! Welcome back to our squad!

(*LU TA-CHENG and the other fighters applaud ardently.*)

(*His uniform and Sten-gun slung over his arms, AH-NAN buries his face in his hands and weeps bitterly.*)

LU TA-CHENG: All right. We're all together once again. If you have some opinions about me just say so. I'm too impatient. You took the angry words I spoke that day to heart, eh? All right, I'm the one who was at fault. After we've finished here, Squad Leader Chao, you call a meeting and let Ah-nan criticize me. I'll attend it and make a self-criticism.

AH-NAN (*sobbing*): No, I'm the one who was wrong. I'm ashamed of myself and feel unable to face you and the rest of the comrades. . . .

HUNG (*going over and wiping away AH-NAN's tears*): Stop crying!

CHAO: Come, you must go and change into your uniform. (*Takes AH-NAN out with the fighters following.*)

LU TA-CHENG: Mama Tung and Uncle Chou, you've taught us a political lesson which is a great help to me as well as to all the fighters. It seems we'll have to ask you to give us lessons regularly. What do you say, Political Instructor?

LU HUA: Right! I support your proposal.

LU TA-CHENG: Uncle Chou, we're the people's own fighters on the Nanking Road. Come and be a political teacher of our men.

CHOU: I'm not qualified.

MAMA TUNG: Instructor! Company Commander! I'm turning my boy over to you.

LU HUA: You don't have to worry, Mama Tung! We'll treat him just like a brother.

CHOU: Let's go.

HUNG: No need to rush. Supper is ready. I want you to have a taste of my cooking. Let's go. We must have some wine, too.

CHOU: Then I'm going to buy some smoked fish.

HUNG: I prepared some fish already. I also prepared dried cakes of bean curd fried with garlic, bean curd garnished with young onions and other dishes. Let's go. (*MAMA TUNG thanks them all. LU TA-CHENG and LU HUA go out with MAMA TUNG and CHOU TEH-KUEI. CHEN HSI is sitting in a corner alone. A short while later, LU TA-CHENG and LU HUA return.*)

LU HUA: Chen Hsi! (*CHEN HSI does not answer.*) Now that Ah-nan has returned to our ranks, you'd better go and see how he's getting along. (*CHEN HSI still doesn't say anything.*)

LU TA-CHENG: Why don't you speak?

CHEN: Please transfer me somewhere to study!

LU TA-CHENG: Are you tired of being a platoon leader?

84

CHEN: I'm not good enough.

(*HUNG MAN-TANG comes back to take away the candies and peanuts.*)

HUNG: Platoon Leader Chen, Ah-nan has already changed into his uniform. You go and have supper with him.

LU TA-CHENG: He's thinking about "quitting"! He wants to retire!

CHEN: Who said I was thinking about "quitting"? I asked to go to study.

HUNG: Study? Where do you want to go to study? Take Nanking Road as your school and study right here. Listen to me, Comrade, because you're ideologically immature the "fragrant" breeze made you lose your balance! (*Starts to go but stops when CHEN HSI speaks.*)

CHEN: Why get angry with me? Why am I blamed for everything? Why are you so polite to Ah-nan and not to me?

LU TA-CHENG (*cutting him short*): We must be stricter with you; we must criticize you!

LU HUA: Do you think the company commander is making a mountain out of a molehill? No! A rotten spot has grown in the back of your mind which is just beginning to show. If we don't point it out to you it will spread all over you.

(*CHEN HSI's eyes show his shock and surprise.*)

LU HUA: Your problem is the most serious in our whole Party branch and company.

HUNG: You. . . . You'd better think this over carefully, Comrade. (*Exit.*)

LU TA-CHENG: I feel sorry for you, Chen Hsi. You can't go on living in your old way. You used to think it didn't matter much if you made minor ideological mistakes so long as you did your duty on the battlefield. When others criticized you they seldom spoke harshly and, paying little attention, you usually ignored them. But the "fragrant" breeze and other things on the Nanking Road make it a breeding ground for men with such weaknesses. All day long you went parading up and down the streets and in the park exchanging autographs and addresses. What was all that for? Dizzy with that girl student's praise, you gave Ah-nan permission to leave his post. You made a big mistake. Old K broke through our line at your position! I don't know how you look at this, but the Instructor and I, after talking things over, think that a Communist must always remember Chairman Mao's injunctions. We must not drop the old tradition of hard work and plain living! (*MESSENGER enters.*)

MESSENGER: Reporting! Company Commander, telephone!

LU TA-CHENG (*begins to go but comes back and takes out a pair of mended cloth socks*): Take off those coloured socks and put on these old cloth ones. They're more durable and will help you to stand steadier on your feet. They served you when we were pulling down the "three big mountains" of imperialism, feudalism and bureaucrat-capitalism; they can serve you now in reforming the Nanking Road.

MESSENGER: You have a phone call from headquarters, Company Commander!

LU TA-CHENG: Your self-criticism had better start from these. (*Pointing to the socks*) You can find the source of your wrong thinking here. (*Exit.*)

(*CHEN HSI takes the socks which he has thrown away.*)

86

LU HUA: Don't think that because we've defeated the enemy with guns everything's over. This is only the first step in a long march of ten thousand *li*. Do you think the colourful city of Shanghai is a place of peace and comfort? Well, it isn't! This is a battlefield of a different type! The enemy's not asleep. The ghost of American imperialism has not yet vanished. It often rides on this "fragrant breeze", hides itself behind clouds, and appears all around us, attacking us under various disguises. Old K is such a ghost. The enemy has never for one moment stopped plotting against us. What you did was to lay down your weapon and surrender!

CHEN: Surrender? (*Glares at LU HUA in surprise.*)

LU HUA: Isn't it surrendering when you throw away your cloth socks, look down your nose at Chao Ta-ta, cold-shoulder Chun-ni and throw away your sewing kit?! What's the difference between that and Tung Ah-nan taking off his uniform and laying down his weapon?

CHEN: I want the Party to punish me!

LU HUA: To punish you is easy, but will it solve the problem? The important thing is to recognize the significance of this struggle. Either we fall here on the Nanking Road or we transform it. This is a life-and-death struggle. . . . Chairman Mao said that "some Communists, who were not conquered by enemies with guns . . . will be defeated by sugar-coated bullets". I've learned a lot from the things that have happened during the last three days. I've gradually come to understand the truth of this statement of Chairman Mao Tsetung's made at the Second Plenary Session of the Seventh Central Committee of the Party. . . . And now

I realize that I also made a mistake for I failed to do my work well for the Third Platoon.

LU HUA (*taking out the sewing kit*): Just before she left, Chun-ni gave me this to keep. I think it's best that I return it to you. It was with you when you marched, fought and performed heroic deeds. Do you still remember you used it to sew up a bullet hole in my uniform when I was hit once. . . . Here take it. Inside is a letter Chun-ni wrote to me. She told me not to let you see it, but I think I should.

(*CHEN HSI takes the sewing kit and fumbles with the letter. The lights are dimmed. A spotlight is on him.*)

THE VOICE OF CHUN-NI: Instructor, I'm very sad, not for myself but for Chen Hsi. Chen Hsi and I, right from our childhood till we joined the revolution, never had a quarrel. I was lucky to have such a husband. Three days after we were married, I went with him to join the People's Liberation Army, which is our own army. When I heard he had been cited for brave deeds in battle, I was inspired to work harder in carrying grain to the front. I never dreamed his way of thinking would change so much after entering the city. And how he has changed! He threw away the cloth socks I made for him and right before my own eyes he threw away the "lovebird" sewing kit that I secretly made for him before we were married. . . . With it he has thrown away the old tradition of the army, Instructor! He has thrown away the kindness of the people in the Liberated Areas! He has thrown away his own glorious record! I feel sorry for him. The Party has educated him all these years. He did not succumb to the enemy's guns but has fallen a victim to the bright lights of the Nanking Road in Shanghai. . . . I'm worried about his future! You've been his good friend all along, Instructor. Give him a helping hand....

(*CHEN HSI weeps and falls down on the table.*)

LU TA-CHENG (*entering hurriedly*): That was headquarters calling just now, Instructor. They said though Old Seven has been caught, Old K is still working on the Lin family. They planned to use Lin Yuan-yuan's relationship with Ah-nan to undermine our unit and take Ah-nan away!

(*The air-raid alarm is sounded.*)

LU TA-CHENG: So they're trying to attack us from both above and below! (*To CHEN HSI*) Comrade, you still have to work hard. The revolution is not over yet! Messenger!

(*The MESSENGER answers and enters.*)

LU TA-CHENG: Notify all posts to tighten up their watch.

(*The MESSENGER goes out.*)

(*CHAO TA-TA leads his squad fully equipped with rifles and packs across the stage.*)

(*In full uniform and carrying a rifle, TUNG AH-NAN dashes in.*)

AH-NAN (*to CHEN HSI*): Tung Ah-nan reporting for duty!

CHEN: Come with me to your post.

(*Exeunt.*)

LU TA-CHENG: The Commander told me over the phone just now that leaders of the Municipal Party Committee are going to attend the celebration in the Park tonight....

(*The stage darkens for a change of scene.*)

SCENE EIGHT

At the entrance to a flower-shop on the Nanking Road.

FEIFEI is standing at a street corner waiting for someone. After a while, CHU MAN-LI comes along carrying a violin case. She hands it to FEIFEI.

FEIFEI: Here are the train tickets you asked me to buy. (*Gives her the tickets.*)

CHU: The thing's inside. Set it for nine thirty. Do a clean job!

FEIFEI: Old K is waiting for you at the Fili Bar.

CHU: I know.

FEIFEI: Someone's following us.

CHU: I can deal with him.

FEIFEI (*taking the hint*): Wait for me a minute, Man-li! (*Goes into the flower-shop.*)

CHU: Hurry up, Feifei!

(*Indifferently, CHEN HSI walks up.*)

CHU: Oho, Platoon Leader Chen!

CHEN: Hello, Man-li.

CHU: What luck! We meet again.

CHEN: It really is luck. What new programme is being put on at the Park tonight?

CHU: Er.... This is the last night of celebration in the Park. There's going to be singing....

90

CHEN: There'll be singing, dancing, rowing on the lake, and story telling. Right?

CHU: Right! And there'll be a solo by Lin Yuan-yuan.

CHEN: Really?

CHU: Can you come?

CHEN: Nothing will stop me.

CHU: Aren't you afraid others will gossip? (*Changing her tone*) Of course, we would welcome you with open arms if you could come.... You're really good at telling stories.

CHEN: Is that so? I'm going to tell the best one I know this time.

CHU: How marvellous! I'll be waiting for you in the same old place.

CHEN: No, I'd like to go along with you now.

CHU: Er... ahem.... Someone's asked me to buy a bouquet for Lin Yuan-yuan. After that I have to see someone.

CHEN: Oh, I see. If that's the case I won't trouble you.

CHU: I'll see you at the Park, eh? Don't disappoint me. I want to hear your best story.

CHEN: All right, I'm going to tell my best story to you alone. Good-bye. (*Waves good-bye and goes out.*) (*CHU MAN-LI goes into the flower-shop smiling. CHAO TA-TA enters. A well-dressed woman carrying parcels of gifts walks across the stage with her husband.*)

WOMAN: What a coincidence! (*Speaking to her husband*) This soldier really....

CHAO: Dark, eh?

WOMAN: Looks smart!

CHAO: Come back! (*Takes out a small purse.*) Is this your purse?

WOMAN: Oh, yes. Thank you. Thank you. (*Sticking up her thumb*) This soldier is really fine! (*Goes out with her husband.*)

(*CHEN HSI enters.*)

CHEN: Keep an eye on that violin case. The stuff might be inside it.

CHAO: Yes.

CHEN: Ask Ah-hsiang what they did in the shop just now.

CHAO: I think we should arrest that woman first....

CHEN: Don't beat the grass and frighten away the snake. Our main target is Old K. Tell Ah-nan to keep his date. He's not to leave Lin Yuan-yuan for one minute.

CHAO: Yes, Platoon Leader! If Ah-nan is not willing I'll go instead.

CHEN: You stand aside! You can't take his place in this. I'm going first. (*Exit.*)

(*CHU MAN-LI and FEIFEI come out of the flower-shop. CHU MAN-LI walks to the left of the stage carrying a bouquet.*)

(*FEIFEI walks to the right of the stage carrying a violin case. CHAO TA-TA suddenly blocks his way.*)

FEIFEI: Hello, Comrade of the Liberation Army! You're doing a good job! I've come to pay you a special visit to express my respect. You've liberated me and lifted me out of my former rotten life. You've helped me to see the light of day. You're really.... (*Singing*) "The sky in the Liberated Areas is bright. The people in the Liberated Areas are happy...."

CHAO: Shut up! (*Pointing to the violin case*) Open it!

FEIFEI: It's a violin. You want to listen to the violin? All right. (*Opens the violin case.*)

(*CHAO TA-TA takes out the violin but sees nothing else.*)

FEIFEI: Want it? I'll give it to you. Take it as a gift from me!

CHAO: Oh no. Let's go and I'll treat you to a drink.

FEIFEI: Some other time. (*Pretends to hiccup.*) . . . I'll go with you to have a drink some other time. . . . (*Staggers.*)

CHAO: What's the matter? Drunk again? (*Bellowing*) Stand still! Ha-ha! You think I'm a greenhorn. Pedicab!

(*With a band bearing the words "People's Guard" round his arm, AH-JUNG runs in.*)

AH-JUNG: Hey, Hooligan, recognize me?

CHAO: Take care of him for me. I'll join you later.

AH-JUNG: Very good! (*To FEIFEI*) Get moving!

CHAO (*pointing to the violin case*): Be careful of that!

AH-JUNG: I know. (*Takes FEIFEI out.*)

(*Coming out of the shop to see her customers off, AH-HSIANG spots CHAO TA-TA.*)

AH-HSIANG: Comrade Chao Ta-ta!

CHAO: How are you?

AH-HSIANG: Fine!

CHAO: Are you busy?

AH-HSIANG: Yes. Don't go away, Comrade Chao Ta-ta. One of those hooligans came into the shop just now and bought a bouquet.

CHAO: And then what did he do?

AH-HSIANG: He opened up his violin case.

CHAO: What for?

AH-HSIANG: To take out a box of resin to give a girl student.

CHAO: What happened next?

93

AH-HSIANG: The girl student put the resin in the bouquet.

CHAO: What kind of flowers were in the bouquet?

AH-HSIANG: White roses.

CHAO: And then what happened?

AH-HSIANG: The girl took the flowers away.

CHAO: Which way did she go?

AH-HSIANG: (*indicating with her hand*): In that direction.

CHAO: Thank you, Ah-hsiang. Good-bye.

AH-HSIANG: What has happened?

CHAO (*leaving*): Things are not so calm on the Nanking Road. We must be vigilant.

(*AH-HSIANG nods and starts to go back to the flowershop.*)

CHAO (*coming back*): Wait a minute, I want to buy a bouquet, too.

AH-HSIANG: You also want a bouquet?

CHAO: Yes.

AH-HSIANG: What kind of flowers?

CHAO: Red roses!

(*Stage darkens for a change of scene.*)

(*At the entrance to the Fili bar. OLD K enters carrying a suitcase. He meets CHU MAN-LI, checks the time, gives her the signal and leaves. LO KE-WEN comes out of the bar a little drunk.*)

CHU: Oh, Mr. Lo!

LO: I'm very pleased to see you, Man-li. You're the only one I feel close to now. Come, let's go dancing.

CHU: You never used to dance, did you? You're drunk, Mr. Lo.

LO: Why not? How many times can one get drunk in a lifetime?

CHU: I know you're drunk because of Lin Yuan-yuan. Let me tell you something: she's still in Shanghai.

LO: She's still in Shanghai? Stop pulling the wool over my eyes.

CHU: It's the truth. She's going to perform at the closing ceremony tonight. It's going to be exciting. I heard the mayor is going to be present. I'll take you there to have some fun and we can also go to see Yuan-yuan. Agreed?

LO: Thanks, but it's not right for me to go there empty-handed. . . .

CHU: Look at this! (*Raises the bouquet of white roses.*)

LO: Oh, they're beautiful! (*Smelling them*) I really needed it, Man-li. I thank you very much for your help.

CHU: I had them ready for you long ago. I think you should take them to the stage personally and present them to her to show your thoughtfulness.

LO: That goes without saying. I'll pluck up my courage. . . . I feel a bit nervous, Man-li. I feel that happiness is coming to me soon!
(*Exeunt.*)
(*CHAO TA-TA and TUNG AH-NAN follow them.*)

CHAO: You go straight to the Park, Ah-nan, and find Lin Yuan-yuan! Don't let her out of your sight for one minute.

AH-NAN: I really don't want to see her again, Squad Leader.

CHAO: This is an order! (*Whispering to him*) Look! Lo Ke-wen has the bouquet now.

AH-NAN: Mm.

CHAO: Here! (*Giving the flowers to AH-NAN*) Switch bouquets with him. Don't frighten Miss Chu.

AH-NAN: Very good. (*Continues to follow them.*)

(*Stage darkens for a change of scene.*)

(*A corner of the Park. LIN YUAN-YUAN is heard singing softly accompanied by a piano. AH-NAN enters carrying a bouquet and stands at the end of a long bench.*)

(*A short while later, LO KE-WEN comes in carrying a bouquet and stands at the other end of the bench. They look at each other for a long time, then sit down on the bench with their backs to each other.*)

(*Silence.*)

AH-NAN: What's your name?

LO: Lo! What's yours?

AH-NAN: Tung. Never expected to run into you in the Park.

LO: And on the same bench. . . .

AH-NAN: So we meet again.

LO: Yes, we meet again!

(*A short pause.*)

AH-NAN (*appreciatively*): That is a beautiful song!

LO: True.

AH-NAN: Is that Lin Yuan-yuan singing?

LO: I don't know.

AH-NAN: Have you come to give her a bouquet?

LO: Yes! Why do you ask?

AH-NAN: Do you like my bouquet? It's red.

LO: Damn your bouquet!

AH-NAN: It's a symbol of a bright future, happiness and peace. Let's swap. . . .

LO: No, thanks. That's quite unnecessary.

AH-NAN: Let's trade! Don't miss this rare opportunity or you will regret it for the rest of your life.

LO: How ridiculous! Please go away. I don't care to sit here with you!

AH-NAN: You're apparently prejudiced against me. But I believe facts will make things clear to you. I hope you won't go on believing rumours and fall for the tricks of scoundrels. Wake up and don't be a fool. Why are you set on going to the United States? Why don't you go to the Park and play your violin for your own people and your motherland?

LO: There you go again! Don't come to me with your propaganda!   Good-bye. (*Stands up and walks away.*)

AH-NAN: Stay where you are, Lo Ke-wen!

LO: What are you up to?

AH-NAN: I want to talk to you.

LO: I don't have time. (*Turns to go.*)

AH-NAN: Don't go away, Lo Ke-wen!

LO: Then you go away and leave me alone!

AH-NAN: I can't leave you. I'm responsible for your safety tonight. Understand?

LO: Absurd! (*Exit.*)

(*A burst of warm applause is heard.*)

AH-NAN: Come back here, Lo Ke-wen!
(*Someone shouts off-stage "The bouquet! The bouquet!"*)
(*AH-NAN looks at the flowers in his hand and hides himself behind the trees.*)
(*CHU MAN-LI enters.*)

CHU (*shouting softly*):   The bouquet! The bouquet! Mr. Lo! The flowers! (*Looks at her watch.*) Damn it!
(*LIN YUAN-YUAN enters.*)

CHU (*going up to meet her*):   Come here, Yuan-yuan. Come and sit here. I didn't know you were going to

97

be first on the programme tonight. You really sang well. Someone is supposed to present a bouquet to you. But he's nowhere to be found. What a joke he's pulling on all of us.

YUAN-YUAN: Never mind. Where are the train tickets you said you would buy for me, Man-li?

CHU: Here they are. (*Taking out the tickets*) Look, two tickets.

YUAN-YUAN: Thank you.

CHU: Wait a minute! Aren't you going to take part in the choral singing at the end? (*LIN YUAN-YUAN nods.*) Is there going to be a curtain call after that?

YUAN-YUAN: I don't want to take part in it. When Ah-nan comes I'm leaving right away!

CHU: Isn't the mayor going to receive the performers after the curtain call? It'll be exciting to be received by the mayor! You'll still have time to catch the train after the reception. . . . But it's not becoming to go on the stage empty-handed. You wait here for me. I'll look for the person who's going to present you with the bouquet. (*Exit.*)

(*TUNG AH-NAN walks over to LIN YUAN-YUAN.*)

AH-NAN: Please accept this bouquet!

YUAN-YUAN (*jumping up and down*): Ah-nan! You're the one. . . . (*Takes the bouquet.*)

AH-NAN: Do you like it?

YUAN-YUAN: I like everything of yours! I didn't know you were waiting for me.

AH-NAN: Yes, I've been waiting for a long time.

YUAN-YUAN: This means you're . . . a true friend. Very well. We'll hurry up, spread our wings and fly to a far-away place.

AH-NAN: But I don't want to "fly" now. I want to come back to earth. To tell the truth, I'm not going anywhere!

YUAN-YUAN: You're joking! Look, I've already got the tickets! (*Giving him the train tickets*) Let's leave right now.

AH-NAN: We're not going anywhere for the moment. (*Tears up the train tickets.*)

YUAN-YUAN: Are you crazy?

AH-NAN: No! I'm awake now. I've returned to my unit. I feel I made a mistake in making friends with you.

YUAN-YUAN: If that's the case, leave me alone.

AH-NAN: I must stay with you for the moment.

YUAN-YUAN: Why stay with someone if it is a mistake? (*Walks away.*)

AH-NAN: Don't move from your seat. I know you won't forgive me, you'll hate and curse me. I will accept the consequences. The instructor's words and the suffering I've seen on the Nanking Road have awakened me. I must remember the past so as not to be ashamed of myself in the future. I'm turning back at this cross-road to make a new start.

YUAN-YUAN: I don't understand what you're talking about!

AH-NAN: You don't understand now, but perhaps you will in the future. The revolution demands that we be firm in our work and struggle because the enemy is still amongst us. But here we are dreaming!

YUAN-YUAN: What are you saying? The enemy is amongst us?

(*Off-stage: LO KE-WEN calls out, "YUAN-YUAN!"*)

AH-NAN: Lo Ke-wen's coming! Please do as I ask you. Change this bouquet for the one he is carrying. (*Withdraws behind the trees.*)

(*LIN YUAN-YUAN stands there in amazement, holding the flowers. LO KE-WEN enters.*)

LO: Yuan-yuan! I've finally found you. Let's make up and forget about the past. Look! Isn't this bouquet beautiful!

(*LO KE-WEN hands LIN YUAN-YUAN the bouquet of white roses. LIN YUAN-YUAN gives him the bouquet of red roses.*)

LO (*looking at the roses*): What is this? To hell with it. (*He throws the red roses down.*) Come, let's go home!

YUAN-YUAN: I can't go. The mayor is going to receive us.

(*Applause is again heard.*)

YUAN-YUAN: The mayor is coming.

LO: All right, I'll go with you.

(*LIN YUAN-YUAN starts to go. AH-NAN steps in their path.*)

AH-NAN (*to YUAN-YUAN*): Give me those flowers!

(*LIN YUAN-YUAN is about to give AH-NAN the bouquet.*)

LO (*stops her while shouting at AH-NAN*): You.... Stop taking advantage of others! Get out of the way!

AH-NAN: Hurry up. Please give it to me, Yuan-yuan!

LO (*standing in his path*): Don't pay any attention to him!

AH-NAN: Give it to me. There's a time-bomb inside. (*Startled, LIN YUAN-YUAN drops the bouquet. AH-NAN picks it up and takes out from the centre of it something about the size of a box of resin.*)

AH-NAN: What's this?

LO: I don't . . . don't know.

YUAN-YUAN: What is that thing?

AH-NAN: It's a time-bomb.

(*LO KE-WEN pulls LIN YUAN-YUAN to him. They stand huddled together behind a bench.*)

AH-NAN: Humph! You must be working in league with them. Do you want to kill your cousin, break up the celebration and create an incident here on the Nanking Road?

LO: No! No! I . . . I . . . . Someone gave me the bouquet! Hurry! Throw it away.

YUAN-YUAN: Be careful, Ah-nan!

AH-NAN: Get out of the way. (*Runs out.*)

YUAN-YUAN: Ah-nan!

(*Off-stage AH-NAN shouts, "Stay back!"*)

YUAN-YUAN (*terrified*): What if something happens to him. . . .

LO (*confessing*): It's my fault! It's all my fault. But I hope. . . . I'll go and see. . . .

YUAN-YUAN: No. Let me go.

(*Off-stage AH-NAN shouts, "Don't come! It's dangerous!"*)

(*LO KE-WEN and LIN YUAN-YUAN cling to each other.*)

(*CHU MAN-LI enters.*)

CHU: Oh! Look how close you two are! Where's the bouquet?

LO: You dog! You traitor!

CHU: Don't make such silly jokes, Mr. Lo!

LO: What did you put in that bouquet?

CHU: Was there something in the bouquet? Aw, Mr. Lo! You're really ungrateful!

LO: Come, let's go to the Security Bureau!

CHU: Stand back! (*Whips out a pistol and walks in the direction taken by AH-NAN.*)

LO: I'll catch this secret agent! (*Blocks her path.*)

(*CHU MAN-LI shoots. LO KE-WEN falls to the ground.*)

YUAN-YUAN (*hurriedly helps him up and calls out*): Catch that secret agent!

(*Just when CHU MAN-LI is about to fire at LIN YUAN-YUAN, a shot from the side knocks the pistol out of her hand. CHEN HSI runs on and puts his foot on the pistol.*)

CHEN (*to CHU MAN-LI*): I didn't break my word, did I? Though I'm a little late I still came in good time to tell the last part of my best story. (*Reciting*) A soldier of the Liberation Army shot the pistol out of her hand. When the soldier levelled his gun at her chest, she obediently stuck up her hands. How is it? Interesting?

CHU: Most interesting!

CHEN: The most interesting part is yet to follow. (*AH-NAN enters.*)

AH-NAN: Reporting! I've removed the fuse from that time-bomb.

YUAN-YUAN: Ah-nan! Lo Ke-wen is wounded.

AH-NAN: What?

CHEN: Rush him to the hospital!

(*AH-NAN carries LO KE-WEN out.*)

CHEN: Did you hear that? Your bomb has been destroyed. It will be difficult for Old K to get away too.

CHU: Old K? (*Smiling ironically*) You can give up hoping to catch him! (*The air-raid alarm is sounded.*)

Do you hear that, Platoon Leader Chen? American planes are just overhead. Go on with your singing and dancing! Ha! Now, you'll never be able to finish your fake celebration in the Park.

CHEN: That's all right! We'll just wait and see. Come this way please. (*Takes CHU MAN-LI off.*)

(*Stage darkens for a change of scene.*)

(*A corridor in the hospital. Quietly sitting on a long high-back bench, LIN YUAN-YUAN has been waiting for a long time. NURSE A passes by. LIN YUAN-YUAN stands up.*)

NURSE A: You can't go in now, Miss Lin!

YUAN-YUAN: Let me go in. It may give him strength.

NURSE A: He's been unconscious ever since he came. We're giving him a blood transfusion.

YUAN-YUAN: A blood transfusion?

NURSE A: Keep calm. Don't get excited.

(*Exit NURSE A.*)

(*LIN YUAN-YUAN stares at the door of the operating room for a long time, quietly crying. LU HUA enters carrying a small leather suitcase and a violin case. Seeing LIN YUAN-YUAN he sits down beside her. LIN YUAN-YUAN turns round, sees LU HUA and lowers her head.*)

LU HUA (*breaking the strained silence*): Is your name Lin Yuan-yuan? We met the night Shanghai was liberated. Am I right? You came to the Nanking Road to welcome us.

(*LIN YUAN-YUAN looks out the window.*)

LU HUA: Have you seen your cousin yet?

YUAN-YUAN (*shaking her head and sighing*): I never thought this would happen to him, but I hope he'll pull through.

LU HUA: Don't worry. The hospital will do all it can to help him recover.

YUAN-YUAN: I'm worried. After all he is my cousin and we used to be good friends. He gave me quite a lot of help in my music studies. But what troubled me was that he became a stumbling block to my progress. I used to think that he concentrated all his efforts on music and stayed away from politics because of his lofty attitude as an artist. I did not know his attitude would lead him onto the path of selfishness. Then he fell for the tricks of the counter-revolutionaries. How horrible and shameful that was! I know I shouldn't be telling you all this right now but I just can't help it. I need your advice.

LU HUA: What advice can I give you? I think you should give me your opinion of the Liberation Army.

YUAN-YUAN: Don't embarrass me, Instructor. I'm ashamed of myself. I've made mistakes in my attitude towards both Ah-nan and the Liberation Army.

LU HUA: That wasn't easy to avoid. On the road to progress a person always suffers some setbacks. In meeting you and your family here on the Nanking Road I've learned a great deal.

YUAN-YUAN: I felt your power through Ah-nan's behaviour.

LU HUA: Is that so?

YUAN-YUAN: Really. Ah-nan's behaviour is something to be admired. He has a fine spirit. As for my cousin his life is valuable, but his soul is horrible.

LU HUA: This is interesting. But I want to argue one point with you. I think his soul can be changed and can become as valuable as his life.

YUAN-YUAN: You have faith in him?

LU HUA: Yes. He proved himself to be brave in the Park, didn't he? We must have faith in our era. In this revolutionary era all patriotic young people will change. You're changing yourself, aren't you?

YUAN-YUAN: I? I feel ashamed because I haven't kept up with the times. I hate myself. I hate the fact that I was born in Shanghai, in such a family and with such a mother and such a cousin!

LU HUA: Your family will not decide what you'll do in life. The main thing is your determination to remould yourself.

YUAN-YUAN: I don't know how, when and where to begin. (*She starts to cry.*)

LU HUA: Begin now!
(*LIN YUAN-YUAN stares at him.*)

LU HUA: You must look at yourself from every angle. You shouldn't put the blame on your family and Shanghai! Don't think that breaking away from your mother, cousin and family means to be revolutionary and everything'll be all right. To be frank, you can't cut yourself off from your history and environment. It's connected with you spiritually in a thousand and one ways. You can't break with it all at once. You should have the courage to join the revolutionary ranks and in the process of remoulding yourself change your environment. That's the only true way to a new life!
(*Silence.*)

LU HUA: There're quite a few fine revolutionary heroines in our ranks who grew out of a polluted environment and yet remained uncontaminated. The first chance I get I'll introduce you to some of them.

YUAN-YUAN (*as if in a trance and speaking softly*): Thank you. . . .

LU HUA: I think you can do anything which others can do. But of course you must be prepared to shed more tears.

(*LIN YUAN-YUAN smiles bashfully.*)

YUAN-YUAN (*after a short pause*): Please help me to leave Shanghai. I can work on a farm or in a factory.

LU HUA: You seem to be very determined! But why give up your piano?

YUAN-YUAN: Music . . . (*smiling*) is too abstract!

LU HUA (*laughing*): You've almost got me there! You see you don't have the right to give it up when the people need it. Am I right? I think music is good; I like it. Didn't Nieh Erh[1] use music to awaken the people and inspire the youth? (*Singing*) "The surging waves continue to swell. Fellow students! Get ready to pull your weight and fight for the nation's fate!" He was calling on the people to stand up and struggle. Wasn't he doing something very practical?

YUAN-YUAN: I'm so fortunate to meet you. I've never heard anyone say what you have said. I never thought you could speak such beautiful language. What shall I do, Instructor?

---

[1] Nieh Erh (1912-35) was a well-known composer and founder of proletarian revolutionary music in China.

LU HUA: Use your singing as a weapon to struggle against the enemy; to call upon the people to advance in face of enemy gunfire, to encourage the people to build a new Shanghai and a new China.

YUAN-YUAN (*tears welling up in her eyes*): I'll follow your instructions.

(*The door to the operation room opens and NURSE A and AH-NAN come out.*)

LU HUA (*moving towards them*): How is he?

AH-NAN: He's all right.

NURSE A: He's come round now.

YUAN-YUAN: It's you.... (*Shakes AH-NAN's hand warmly.*)

AH-NAN (*to YUAN-YUAN*): He called your name and said something about a violin.

LU HUA: All are here. Let's go in and see him.

(*LU HUA takes LIN YUAN-YUAN by the arm and goes into the operation room.*)

(*MRS. LIN enters.*)

MRS. LIN: How is Lo Ke-wen, Nurse?

NURSE A: Shh! (*Shakes her head and goes into the room.*)

AH-NAN: He's all right.

MRS. LIN: You're here, too. I've finally found out who you are. You caused the break-up of my family and also let this happen to Lo Ke-wen. (*Weeps.*)

AH-NAN: Mrs. Lin!

MRS. LIN: All right, I have nothing more to say. I believe few soldiers in the Liberation Army are like you. When you go back, please tell the soldier who saved Lo Ke-wen's life that I have great respect for him. If it hadn't been for him I don't know what might have happened to Ke-wen. I admire such soldiers of the Liberation Army, but you....

AH-NAN (*at a loss for words*): All right. Good-bye! (*Exit.*)

(*NURSE A takes LO KE-WEN out of the operation room on a wheel chair. LU HUA and LIN YUAN-YUAN follow.*)

MRS. LIN (*stepping forward*): Ke-wen!

(*LO KE-WEN smiles.*)

NURSE A: Lucky that soldier of the Liberation Army saved him and gave some blood for a transfusion. (*Wheels LO KE-WEN out.*)

MRS. LIN: The Communist Party is great, Instructor. I give in. What's the name of that comrade? I shall pay him a visit.

LU HUA: His name is Tung Ah-nan.

MRS. LIN (*flabbergasted*): What? Tung Ah-nan?

(*The stage darkens for a change of scene.*)

SCENE NINE

*The scene is the same as Scene Seven. It is autumn.
A holiday atmosphere prevails. Hanging from the
balcony is a banner bearing the words: "Resist U.S.
aggression and aid Korea; Protect our homes and
defend our country."*

*CHEN HSI is sitting in a grove making a pair of
cotton-padded gloves.*

*HUNG MAN-TANG quietly makes his way over to
greet CHEN HSI.*

HUNG: Chen Hsi, someone's here to see you off!
CHEN: Who?
HUNG: Our model worker, Chun-ni!
CHEN: She'll never come.
HUNG: Do you think she's like you!
  (*CHUN-NI enters carrying a basket of apples.*)
HUNG: Look, who's this?
CHEN: Chun-ni!
HUNG: All right, I've done my part. Now I'll go
  and cook something for you. (*Exit.*)
CHEN: You really have come?
CHUN-NI: Didn't you expect me?
CHEN: I never dreamed you'd come. Who wrote and
  told you about it?
CHUN-NI: The instructor and Uncle Hung. (*Silence.
  CHEN HSI continues to make the gloves. CHUN-NI*

takes the gloves and needle from him.) Whose gloves
are these?

CHEN: Ah-nan's. (*Silence. CHEN HSI pours out a glass of water for CHUN-NI.*)

CHUN-NI: Where's the thread?
(*CHEN HSI takes from his pack the sewing kit CHUN-NI gave him and goes over to her.*)

CHEN: Here.
(*CHUN-NI stares at the sewing kit.*)

CHEN: Here take it. The instructor returned it to me.
(*CHUN-NI throws the sewing kit down to the floor.*)

CHEN: Now look at you. (*Picks up the sewing kit, beats it with his hand and blows off the dust.*) I'm taking it to the front with me. (*CHEN HSI takes out a thread and gives it to CHUN-NI.*) Go ahead. Get it off your chest. Criticize me, curse me if you like.

CHUN-NI: I didn't come here to settle scores with you.

CHEN: In my heart. . . .

CHUN-NI: You're very cruel!

CHEN: Why do you say that?

CHUN-NI: Why did you go away without writing to me?

CHEN: I thought I'd wait till I arrived in Korea before I wrote to you.

CHUN-NI: Did you think I'd try to stop you from going?

CHEN: I thought that if I waited till I was in Korea before I admitted my mistakes to you, criticized myself and sent you reports of our victories you'd be more willing to forgive me.

CHUN-NI: I hate you! (*Buries her face in CHEN HSI's chest and weeps.*)

CHEN: The lessons that I've learned here on the Nanking Road during the past year are enough to last me a lifetime. You can rest assured I won't do anything to disgrace the Party, my company or you, Chun-ni.

CHUN-NI: Who's asked you to swear an oath? You're doing something much better than I — you're going to fight the U.S. imperialists! I feel honoured that you can go before me. I only regret we've spent so little time together. . . .

(*CHAO TA-TA enters. When he sees the situation, he puts his helmet over his face, turns back and runs a few paces.*)

CHUN-NI: Don't go away, Chao Ta-ta! (*Gives him some apples.*)

CHAO: What am I to do, Platoon Leader?

CHEN: Take them of course. Try one and see if it's good.

CHAO: (*Takes a bite.*) Mm, very good — very sweet.

CHUN-NI: You're leaving with Chen Hsi, aren't you?

CHAO: Yes! The Platoon Leader and I seem to be meant to work together. We crossed the Yangtse together and we came to the Nanking Road together. Now we're going to cross the Yalu together. You can rest assured that after we get to Korea, we shall report our victories to you and the people in the old Liberated Areas.

CHUN-NI: Its very good of you to think of us.

(*AH-NAN enters.*)

AH-NAN: Reporting! I'm all ready!

CHEN: Good.

CHUN-NI (*holding up the gloves*): Put them on, Ah-nan, and see the Platoon Leader's needle-work.

AH-NAN (*saluting*): Thank you.

III

CHUN-NI: Why thank me?

AH-NAN: You've taught our Platoon Leader how to sew and now he's teaching us. (*Takes out his sewing kit.*) Look, I'm taking this to Korea with me to remember you by, Chun-ni.

(*LU TA-CHENG enters.*)

CHEN (*commanding*): Attention!

(*CHEN HSI, CHAO TA-TA and AH-NAN fall into formation.*)

LU TA-CHENG: You're looking fine. All of you look high-spirited and stout of heart. Step over here, Ah-nan. I know I have got a loud voice and because of it I might have given you the shivers.

AH-NAN: Yes. Though you scared me at first, I shall always be thinking of your instructions.

LU TA-CHENG: You also made me feel rather scared at first. (*Takes a pair of cloth shoes out of his leather case.*) Sit down there and change into this pair of shoes.

AH-NAN: Company Commander. . . .

LU TA-CHENG: This pair of shoes was given to me on the battlefield by my squad leader when I was just a recruit. He charged the enemy barefooted and gave his life in that battle. I've kept them all the time, hating to wear them. . . . Now, you're going to fight the U.S. aggressors and help the Koreans. Put them on before you set out to fight the imperialists.

AH-NAN (*accepting the shoes*): I shall always remember your instructions, Company Commander.

(*LU HUA enters surrounded by a group of fighters.*)

LU HUA (*smiling gently*): Now that you're leaving, Ah-nan, our company and Party branch also want to offer you a gift. We have decided to make it known to you on the eve of your departure that you've been admitted into the Youth League.

(*All clap ardently.*)

AH-NAN: But I'm still not qualified to join the Youth League, Instructor.

LU HUA: It happened like this, Comrades. (*Takes out three crumpled applications and a neatly folded one.*) One year ago, Ah-nan wrote an application to join the Youth League. On the back of it, he wrote: "I've forgotten what happened on the Nanking Road in the past. I'm not qualified to be a fighter." So he threw it away. Three months later he wrote another one and on the back of it he wrote: "Why do I try to get away from the Nanking Road? Since I have fallen down here I should try to stand up here but I have not got the courage. I'm not qualified to join the Youth League with such a problem." He threw that one away too. He wrote a third application three months later and on the back of it he wrote: "I can't compare with my Platoon Leader or Squad Leader, to say nothing about comparing with the Old Mess Officer. I can't join the Youth League." He threw that one away too. He handed in only this fourth application to the Youth League. On it he wrote: "I shall always heed the words of Chairman Mao and follow the Party. I'll dedicate my youth and my whole life to the cause of communism." Having considered Comrade Ah-nan's demand and determination to join the revolution, and observed his behaviour, the Youth League decided to admit him. (*All applaud enthusiastically.*) You should keep these three crumpled copies of your application, Ah-nan. They are the most significant records of your life.

AH-NAN (*solemnly accepting the three crumpled copies of his application*): You know everything, Instructor.

LU TA-CHENG: The instructor went behind you picking them up as you threw them away. He knows the whole story.

(*HUNG MAN-TANG, greatly moved, wipes away his tears.*)

LU TA-CHENG: What's wrong, Old Hung? (*Also wiping his tears away.*)

HUNG: I can't stop you now. Your wings have grown strong and you're going to fly away. The Nanking Road is changing and so is our company. We have successors to our cause now. If you ever need my services when you get to Korea just send me a message. I can carry kitchen pots for you if nothing else.

LU HUA: Comrades! You're going to Korea and we're staying here on the Nanking Road; but our target is the same: to carry the revolution through to the end! Chen Hsi! (*CHEN HSI and CHAO TA-TA step forward.*) You two are veterans. You must take care of Ah-nan on the way.

CHEN }
CHAO } : Yes!

AH-NAN: Instructor, now that I'm about to leave the Nanking Road, let me stand guard here for the last time.

LU HUA: All right.

(*The stage darkens for a change of scene.*)

EPILOGUE

Neon lights bearing the words "Long Live the People's Republic of China!" and "Long Live Chairman Mao!" flash on and off.

AH-NAN stands guard in combat dress.

AH-JUNG, newly enlisted, enters to relieve AH-NAN.

AH-JUNG: Chou Ah-jung reporting for duty.

AH-NAN: What's our task?

AH-JUNG: To hold our post and defend Shanghai. Good-bye.

AH-NAN: Good-bye.

(AH-JUNG walks to his post.)

(LU HUA enters carrying AH-NAN's pack and walking along with CHEN HSI and CHAO TA-TA. The MESSENGER follows them. LU TA-CHENG and HUNG MAN-TANG walk along hand in hand with the fighters who are leaving.)

AH-NAN: Instructor, please don't go any further.

LU HUA: Let me walk along this road with you once more.

(LIN YUAN-YUAN enters.)

YUAN-YUAN: Ah-nan! Wait a minute!

AH-NAN *(turning round)*: Yuan-yuan, it's you!

YUAN-YUAN: Are you going to Korea?

AH-NAN *(nodding)*: Yes!

YUAN-YUAN: You move so fast I can't keep up with you. (*Gives him a notebook.*) Keep this as a souvenir. I'm trying to join the Army's Song and Dance Ensemble. We may see each other again.

AH-NAN: See you at the front!

(*CHUN-NI enters carrying a basket of apples.*)

CHUN-NI: Here are some apples from my home town; take them along with you.

(*MRS. LIN and LO KE-WEN enter. LO KE-WEN shakes hands with TUNG AH-NAN.*)

MESSENGER: They've come, Instructor.

(*The beat of drums is heard. Gathered around MAMA TUNG, AH-HSIANG and CHOU TEH-KUEI, the fighters enter. AH-HSIANG gives CHAO TA-TA a bouquet.*)

MAMA TUNG (*going over to her son*): Ah-nan! It's cold up north. Take this fur-lined vest with you. Don't ever forget that your father shed his blood on the Nanking Road!

CHOU: Comrades! The trade union has sent me here as its representative for two purposes: One is to see the comrades off to resist U.S. aggression and aid Korea. The second is to welcome the comrades who are going to continue to guard the Nanking Road and defend socialist construction in the motherland. On behalf of all the workers on the Nanking Road, I express our highest tribute to you. (*Unfolds a banner bearing the words "People's soldiers guarding the Nanking Road".*)

(*Ceremoniously the troops accept the banner.*)

LU HUA: Mama Tung! Uncle Chou! It's to your credit and to the credit of the Shanghai working class that we have such good soldiers as these.

116

MAMA TUNG: Credit goes to all of you and Chairman Mao!

   (*Artillery salute is heard.*)

LU TA-CHENG: The fireworks have already started. Are you ready, Comrades?

AH-NAN (*saluting*):   Good-bye!

   (*The fighters march out.*)

   (*LIN YUAN-YUAN, CHUN-NI and AH-HSIANG wave them good-bye.*)

   (*CHOU TEH-KUEI and MAMA TUNG wave.*)

   (*Many other people come up to see them off.*)

   (*A group of Liberation Army soldiers march by under the bright lights, singing together.*)

CURTAIN